MW00943485

"Kelsey Phillips' *College Bo*
insight based on her life-long commitment to teenage girls. By
sharing her own experiences and real-life examples, Kelsey
becomes the guide who points out the ups and downs of college
life. *College Bound on Solid Ground* is a gift and a blessing to
all students!"

Jay Lee
Pastor to College & Young Adults
Highland Park Presbyterian Church, Dallas, TX

"*College Bound on Solid Ground* is an absolute must-read for
every young woman making the precarious transition from
high school to college. It is written with unparalleled poignancy
and relevancy by a woman who has successfully traversed this
journey with grace and wisdom beyond her years, and it gives
tremendous practical advice to everyone wanting to succeed,
both spiritually and otherwise, during their college years!"

Ashley Joseph
Professional Baseball Wives Ministries

"College is the proving ground for every conviction, every
belief system you as a young adult claim to possess. How you
prepare for it will ultimately determine who you will become.
With an insightful balance of academia and the practical,
Kelsey Phillips gives you lasting tools for this exciting yet
more-than-challenging time. The leverage of this book for me,
however, rests in its voice. I have known Kelsey since she was
a freshman in high school. Perhaps the greatest thing I could
ever say about Kelsey is this: I pray my two daughters grow
up to be young women like her."

Stuart Hall
Rethink Group & Dash Inc
Coauthor / Seven Checkpoints for Students
& Max Q: Developing Students of Influence

"In today's explosion of information, few books break new ground, but Kelsey Phillips has done just that in *College Bound on Solid Ground*. This is a must read book for graduating seniors and college students."

Dr. Fred Lowery
Sr. Pastor of First Baptist Bossier, Bossier City, Louisiana
Author / Making the Bible Clear & Covenant Marriage

COLLEGE BOUND
on
SOLID GROUND

A GIRL'S GUIDE TO SURVIVING AND THRIVING IN COLLEGE

COLLEGE BOUND
on
SOLID GROUND

KELSEY TEMPLE PHILLIPS

Pleasant Word
A Division of WINEPRESS PUBLISHING

Pleasant Word (a division of WinePress Publishing, PO Box 428, Enumclaw, WA 98022) functions only as book publisher. As such, the ultimate design, content, editorial accuracy, and views expressed or implied in this work are those of the author.

Unless otherwise noted, all Scriptures are taken from the *Holy Bible, New International Version*®, niv®. Copyright © 1973, 1978, 1984 by the International Bible Society. Used by permission of Zondervan. All rights reserved.

Scripture quotations marked msg are from *THE MESSAGE*. Copyright © by Eugene H. Peterson 1993, 1994, 1995, 1996, 2000, 2001, 2002. Used by permission of NavPress Publishing Group.

Scripture quotations marked kjv are taken from the *King James Version* of the Bible.

Scripture quotations marked nlt are taken from the *Holy Bible, New Living Translation,* copyright © 1996. Used by permission of Tyndale House Publishers, Inc., Wheaton, IL 60189 USA. All rights reserved.

ISBN 13: 978-1-4141-1154-4
ISBN 10: 1-4141-1154-1
Library of Congress Catalog Card Number: 2007909770

Remember your Creator during your youth: when all possibilities lie open before you and you can offer all your strength intact for his service. The time to remember is not after you become senile and paralyzed! Then it is not too late for your salvation, but too late for you to serve as the presence of God in the midst of the world and the creation. You must take sides earlier—when you can actually make choices, when you have many paths opening at your feet, before the weight of necessity overwhelms you.

—Jacques Ellul
Reason for Being:
A Meditation on Ecclesiastes[1]

CONTENTS

Part Two—Growing in the Physical Life

Part Three—Growing in the Spiritual Life

Part Four—Growing in the Social Life

ACKNOWLEDGMENTS

I have learned that it takes many people to navigate this writing and publishing journey from beginning to end. Without these wonderful friends the Lord put on my path, this book for sure would have never been completed.

To my friends at Parkhill Junior High and the New Jersey Writing Project Texas team in the Richardson Independent School District: thank you for setting the foundation and providing me the professional tools that equipped me for this project.

To Emily Wilkinson and the youth and college staff at Highland Park Presbyterian Church: thank you for allowing me the opportunity to learn from you, glean your wisdom, and become partners with you in College Bound.

To those diligent friends (Ruth Cooper, Stuart Hall, Ashley Joseph, Debbie Keys, Ashley Knee, Jay and Lee Sun Lee, Leigh-Baskin McConnell, Jill Scovell, Ann Temple, and Leslie Temple) that read this in its earliest form, gave priceless advice, and provided much needed fine tuning: thank you for your precious time.

To the wonderful high school senior girls I have been honored and delighted to disciple these past few years in the Dallas area: thank you for teaching me more than I could have ever taught you.

To Ruth: this all started because of your boldness for the Lord and desire to grow in Him during your college years. Thank you for being the very first guinea pig!

To the team at Pleasant Word: thank you for such a smooth ride for a first-timer.

To my supportive friends and family who have listened, loved, and prayed over this book from start to finish: thank you from the bottom of my heart.

To my incredible husband, Chandler: thank you for your unconditional support, solid advice, editor's eye, and allowing me to pursue a dream.

To my Lord: this is for you – all of it.

INTRODUCTION

The fat packet has finally arrived in the mail—you did it. A swirling wind of new uncertainties and overwhelming feelings hits now that you have officially been accepted into college. Housing applications, orientation sessions, sorority deadlines. You thought the stress was over, but now you feel like it has begun all over again. It's just a guess, but this anxiety may be because you are sensing that college is more than just an academic experience… and you are right.

You are most likely prepared for the academic life in college (although this book will address that, in case you are still nervous about it). You may think preparations began your freshman year of high school when grades permanently tattooed themselves on your high school transcript. But actually, it started even before then. In 2001, the American Council of Education published an extensive academic report titled *The School to College Transition*, stating that "Students must begin to develop college awareness and aspirations in the middle-school years in order to take algebra and other gate-keeping courses, which then position students for high school coursework that aligns well with college enrollment courses."[2] That means you were officially preparing for college as early as *seventh grade*! As a former middle-school teacher in Texas public schools, I was a part of that system that had to broach the big, scary word "college" to terrified twelve- and thirteen-year-olds during their seventh grade year. As an English teacher and writing coach, I spent my days preparing these students academically for their distant yet eagerly anticipated college years.

Needless to say, I'm fairly confident you've spent the past six years (at the minimum) making academic preparations to equip yourself with the tools needed to tackle the challenging college curriculum awaiting you. Have you also been preparing for the physical, social, and spiritual challenges on the horizon? Hopefully the answer is yes. Parents, families, churches, youth groups, friends, camps, mentors, organizations, and even extracurricular activities such as sports could have played a role in helping mold and shape the faith, character, and values that you do or don't have at this point in your life. Regardless, they will all be tested during this next phase called college.

This book is designed to help prepare you to grow academically, physically, spiritually, and socially in proper balance during the next four years. It is based on the Bible verse Luke 2:52: "And Jesus grew in wisdom and stature, and in favor with God and men." To my knowledge, there is no scriptural evidence of what Jesus was doing in life from the time He was a boy teaching in the temple (Luke 2:42-50) to the time He began ministering publicly at age thirty (Luke 3:23) other than this verse. If I'm doing my math correctly, that means between the ages of twelve and thirty, our Lord and Savior was growing in wisdom (honoring God with his mind—academic life), growing in stature (honoring God with his strength—physical life), growing in favor with God (honoring God with his soul—spiritual life), and growing in favor with man (honoring God with his heart—social life). All of this was preparing and equipping Him for the world-changing events that would occur during His three-year ministry before His ultimate sacrificial death. Darrel Bock, author of the gospel commentary *Jesus, According to Scripture,* said, "Wisdom, stature, and favor with both God and people reveal Luke's very human portrait of Jesus."[3] If we are to model our lives after Christ, what better way to spend our time between our elementary years and the real world than also growing in those four areas?

As college brings you to a clear transition from childhood to young adulthood, these pages will challenge you to pursue the very things Christ did.

I'm not alone in presenting these four key areas as the four pillars of balance in approaching life. The Center for Parent and Youth Understanding (CPYU) has launched its own research project called the College Transition Initiative hoping to find better ways to equip high school students for all the components the college transition brings. In his article "Navigating the College Transition," Derek Melleby, director of the College Transition Initiative, challenges high school students to ask themselves four crucial questions before taking off for their college destination:

1. Why am I going to college?
2. Who am I?
3. What do I believe?
4. With whom will I surround myself?[4]

My hope is that this book will help you think through these four key questions, along with many others, before taking the college plunge. Think of these four components as the four "legs" holding up a sturdy table. What goes on top of the table will be greatly influenced by the strength of the four legs. If a balance of these four areas (the academic life, the physical life, the spiritual life, and the social life) is fervently pursued during college, then you are setting a solid foundation for a balanced life that will carry you on for the rest of your life. Steven Garber, a college professor and author of *The Fabric of Faithfulness,* puts it this way:

For those whose pathway leads them into the world of university, decisions are made during that time that are determinative for the rest of life. In the modern world, the years between eighteen and twenty-five are a time for the settling of one's convictions about meaning and morality: Why do I get up in the morning? What do I do after I get up in the morning? One then settles into life with those convictions as the shaping presuppositions and principles of one's entire life.[5]

As college could be the first major transition in your life, having the discipline and accountability to keep these four areas in check will make the next transition (moving from college to the real world) even smoother.

My Story

Perhaps like some of you, I grew up in the church—a small-town, Louisiana kind of church. My family went to Sunday school each Sunday, and I participated in every choir, vacation Bible school, youth group, and church camp event that the church provided. Ironically, though, it wasn't until my junior year of high school that I realized I didn't have my own personal relationship with Jesus Christ. Fighting the pride in me that didn't want to reveal to my friends and peers that I didn't *really* know God, I finally broke down one night during summer church camp, walked down that isle, and gave my life to Jesus. I'll never forget that night. A warm sensation covered my body and calmed my ferociously beating heart as I felt this new peace take over all my anxieties and hurts. Not long after that, Satan was at work filling me full of doubt and fear, and bringing a new set of temptations into my life to distract me from God's plan.

A year later, I was making preparations to attend Texas A&M University. God used those college years to strengthen my faith, bring purpose to my pains, and introduce me to a whole new world of Christian community. With a wealth of wonderful friends, a refined faith, and a scrapbook full of fun memories, I graduated in the year 2000 with a degree in education and set off to the big city to change the world one student at a time. I would not have been spiritually prepared for the challenges that come along with working in the "real world" had my faith not been refined and sharpened during those college years. I did not realize it at the time, but looking back I now see how the Lord divinely placed people in my path who challenged me in the areas of my academic life, my physical life, my spiritual life, and my social life. Because college had such a powerful impact on me, my hope and prayer is to present you with what college can offer you. No campus is exactly the same, but Hebrews 13:8 tells us, "Jesus Christ is the same yesterday and today and forever." And Jeremiah 29:11 reveals that His plan for you is perfect and pure. Most adults will tell you that college is a "make it or break it" experience when it comes to finding out who you are and what you believe. I hope these pages present encouragement, personal challenges, practical information, and food for thought as you enter this new world.

How This Book Came About

A couple of years ago, I was out of college and struggling with the transition between school and the real world. God used the scripture in Luke 2:52, "And Jesus grew in wisdom and stature and in favor with God and men," to give me direction, peace, and a more balanced view of how to approach life as a single working girl. It revealed that even Jesus had a season where he had to grow in the areas of the mind, the body, the heart, and the soul. This showed me that God desires a healthy balance in all these areas. I realized I had allowed the stress of my first "real" job to get me out of balance.

God planted a seed in my heart during that time that I was not the only one struggling with "transitions." During those early, tough years teaching in the public classroom, I had no idea that God would bring a life-changing student across my path. Through a series of what I call "God events," a bold young ninth-grader named Ruth discovered I was a Christian and asked me to mentor her. Accepting the offer to be her "Paul," as she called it, we began meeting every other week for the next four years, talking about everything you can imagine and more. As Ruth approached her senior year, God allowed me the opportunity to prepare her for her college experience using the same verse and principles now before you in this book. I am forever grateful to Ruth for allowing me to be a part of her life and for being a "guinea pig" her senior year, testing out these ideas. Her encouragement, passion, and devotion to her Savior are a few of the reasons this project is finally complete. Ruth is now attending Texas A&M University and changing that campus one student at a time.

Not long after Ruth graduated, my husband and I started volunteering with the youth at our church. I naturally gravitated to the high school senior girls, where I joined a long-time friend from college (who had been teaching and challenging senior girls for years) to help co-lead a senior girls' Bible study. Week by week, we dove into Scripture and talked candidly and honestly about the hot topics college was about to bring. From that Bible study, word spread in the community, and God opened a door for me to teach and disciple seniors from many churches in the Dallas area. The material that evolved over those years has become this book. What a joy it has been watching these remarkable young women become greatly successful in college. I'm blessed and honored to now share in this exciting journey with you!

How This Book Works

This book is not a recipe, but rather a guide to bring awareness of tough college issues to the surface for you to consider before going off on your own. It can be read on your own from beginning to end, in portions as you see fit, or in a small group setting filled with discussion. Within four, clearly-organized sections you will find chapters that contain quick-reads about common college topics, questions for reflection, and a digging deeper section to help you navigate through scripture pertaining to each topic.

The first major section discusses the first area in Luke 2:52—wisdom. In this next phase of life, wisdom will be most overtly handed to you in the traditional college setting of class lectures and through your own reading assignments. The first section helps you approach the technical and practical side of honoring God with your mind in the academic arena of college.

The next area that Jesus grew in was stature. The second section brings out an understanding that our bodies are a temple of God and the importance of learning how to properly take care of it for the first time on your own. Each chapter in this section addresses different ways you can honor God with your strength as you physically grow during college.

Growing in favor with God is the third area in which Jesus pursued growth. God wants to know us intimately and personally. The Bible is full of God's promises for our lives, but we must seek Him first. He wants to be the number one priority in our lives above all else. The third section articulates how you can honor God with your soul through your spiritual life.

Finally, Jesus grew in favor with man. This is not to imply that he *sought* the favor of man, but rather that he grew socially and learned how to interact, love, and communicate effectively with others—and most importantly, how to serve them. During this coming social prime of your life, honoring God with all your heart will allow your social life to thrive greatly.

It is no surprise that in light of God's design for perfect harmony in all these areas as seen in the Garden of Eden, Satan has a different plan for us. First Peter 5:8 warns us to "Be self-controlled and alert. Your enemy the devil prowls around like a roaring lion looking for someone to devour." Satan is looking for ways to steal our joy in life and connection to all truth. Satan will lurk to find weaknesses in our sinful nature that pervert what God created to distract us from God's ultimate calling in our lives. The image that comes to mind is a broken leg on our four-legged table. If that happens, the table is no longer stable, but on shaky support. The enemy wants nothing more than for us to get out of balance and obsess more on one area than the others to keep us from that perfect harmony. Ultimately, living in balance allows us to not only know God, but it also allows us to bless others through Him. Each section will warn of potential weak areas or strongholds that allow Satan to destroy, distort, and pervert this balance. When this happens, God, in His unlimited mercy and grace, will always welcome us back with open arms and somehow fix our broken table. The good news is that we know through the book of Revelation that one day Satan will ultimately be beaten and God's people will live with Him for eternity in effortless, pure harmony.

In answer to the question of which all of God's commandments was the most important, Jesus says in Mark 12:30, "'Love the Lord your God with all your heart and with all your soul and with all your mind, and with all your strength.' The second is this: 'Love your neighbor as yourself.' There is no commandment greater than these." I invite you now to take a deeper look at how that plays out on a college campus. Oh, and by the way, no one ever achieves this delicate balance here on earth. As Ecclesiastes 11:7-10 says, life is a journey to enjoy, and we learn as we go. Are you ready for the ride?

Chapter 1

THE BIG TRANSITION

Trust in the Lord with all your heart and lean not on your own understanding; in all your ways acknowledge him, and he will make your paths straight.

—Proverbs 3:5-6

Transition is just a fancy word for change. If you think about it, you've experienced a good handful of transitions in your life already. Your parents will never forget the day they gleefully cheered you on as you stumbled through your first steps and kissed crawling goodbye. You'll never forget that first day of junior high when you couldn't get your locker open, and you missed "homeroom" class for the first time. And I'm almost positive you and your parents distinctly remember the day you roared out of the driveway without having to ask

1

for a ride—fully embracing the new freedom of your own driver's license (and possibly a totaled mailbox). All these represent life experiences that required a transition away from life as you knew it in order to get to the next place (even if it was scary at first).

I believe that one *major* transition in a young woman's life is leaving the well-known comforts of home (after finally getting the hang of high school) and all of a sudden having a credit card, roommate, and nobody to check in with at the end of the night. The way you spend these precious years called college can either serve as the biggest blessing or biggest struggle as you enter the real world a little further down the road.

For most college-bound students, this leap is scary for one of two main reasons. Either you've enjoyed high school and you are fearful of leaving your group of friends, your boyfriend, and your comfortable place in this world, or you are ready to be finished with it altogether and looking for a fresh start (which means going to a new place where you don't know anyone). Both reasons have natural anxieties attached to them. Abbie Smith says it best in her creative book *Can You Keep Your Faith in College?* She opens her first chapter with, "Seems like there are two kinds of transitioners: One loved high school and is scared to death of college, and the other is sick of high school and ready for something new."[6] Regardless of which category you fall under, you are not alone in having these legitimate fears

2

and desires when transitioning from high school to college.

This transition is a big deal, especially when it is estimated that only 25 percent of youth group kids continue to go to church when they get to college.[7] This statistic raised serious concern for the Center for Youth and Family Ministry (CYFM) at Fuller Seminary. With a passion to see more students bridge a healthy gap between high school and college, this organization has spearheaded a three-year research project called the *College Transition Project*. The goal of this project is to first "better understand what happens to students when they transition from youth group life into college/young adult life. And second...to see what parts of the youth group life seem to be associated with a healthy, positive, transition into college life."[8]

The initial phase of this project, which began in 2004, surveyed a number of students who had been a part of their local youth ministries during their high school years and had moved on to college. According to Kara Powell, director of CYFM, the research completed thus far has revealed the top three most difficult elements of their transition to be:

1.   making friends and finding a community,
2.   being alone for the first time and having to bear certain responsibilities, and finally
3.   finding a church or spiritual community in which they felt comfortable and welcome.[3]

The same survey reported that 69 percent of students had been sexually active and 100 percent of those surveyed had used alcohol not long after entering the college scene.[3] Let me repeat myself…this transition is a big deal. And along with the visionaries of the College Transition Project, I also want to help you make this transition as smoothly and healthily as possible.

Luke 2:52 states, "And Jesus grew in wisdom and stature, and in favor with God and men." Even Jesus had a season in His life when He was preparing Himself in wisdom (pursuing knowledge of the world around Him), stature (pursuing strength in His physical body), growing in favor with God (pursuing a more intimate relationship with the Lord), and favor with man (pursuing meaningful relationships with people).

You are about to enter a season of your life that was specifically designed for this purpose, and what better way to spend your time in college than pursuing the same sense of balance Jesus Himself pursued when He was your age? My prayer is that in these pages you will find practical ways to fully engage in an exciting college experience that will allow you to grow mentally, physically, spiritually, and socially, regardless of what team you are cheering for during the next four (or five, or six) years of your life!

Chapter One Reflection Questions

1. What are some of the biggest transitions you have experienced in your life so far?

2. Which category do you fall under right now: the one who loves high school and doesn't want to leave or the one who is done with high school and can't wait to start over?

3. Have you prayed about where to go to college?

Digging Deeper

■ Luke 2:52 reveals the four areas of balance to pursue:

1. _____ in college known as _____.

2. _____ in college known as _____.

3. _____ in college known as _____.

4. _____ in college known as _____.

■ Review again Luke 2:52. Write down good habits you acquired in those four areas during high school that you want to take with you to college. Now write down unhealthy habits in those four areas you would like to try to break.

■ Why does God desire for us to seek Him and His will for our lives during our youth?

- Lamentations 3:25

- Ecclesiastes 12:1-14

Chapter 2

. . . .

HIGH SCHOOL SENIOR YEAR– BETWEEN TWO WORLDS

However, I consider my life nothing to me, if only I may finish the race and complete the task the Lord has given me—the task of testifying to the gospel of God's grace.

—Acts 20:24

Ever heard of senioritis? This is the time during your senior year when that final homecoming game is over, the last football pep rally has passed, prom is around the corner, and college is all the talk at school. I distinctly remember that point in my senior year when all the "coolness" of being at the top was wearing off and getting to the finish line was all I cared about. Senioritis is such a widespread academic problem that the Department of Education launched what's called *The Commission on the High School Senior Year* because "students seem to lose interest in school by their senior year and do not use it effectively as a time of transition to life after compulsory schooling."[9]

I'd like to tell you Addie's story. Addie loved to cheer. Her high school years outside of class time revolved around cheerleading practices, competitions, and private lessons. When the time came for Addie to try out for the varsity team at her high school her junior year, she did not make the squad. Devastated but determined, Addie kept on with her other competitive squad and private lessons. Another year rolled around, and it was the last opportunity for Addie to make varsity. Confident that she had properly prepared as much as she knew how while fully trusting the Lord with the outcome, she gave it all she had and tried out one last time. This time, she made the squad. It did not take Addie long to figure out why God had orchestrated these events in the order that He did. She found herself a beacon of hope and positive leadership amongst a group of girls who complained about everything. From long practices, to cold football evenings, Addie felt blessed to even be on the field—she kept the squad spirits up and challenged them to have a good attitude in all circumstances. The little things that became pet peeves to those who had cheered varsity before were new and fresh to Addie. When senioritis started setting in with the seniors on the squad, Addie was the first to stand up and not allow laziness or apathy to enter their team.

Addie could have easily given up when she didn't make it her junior year and used her senior year to slack off and breeze by. Instead, Addie became an example to all those around her of how persistence and determination pay off in the face of adversity, how keeping a positive attitude is essential in all circumstances, and most of all...how to finish strong.

In what areas of your life are you going to stay determined and positive and finish strong your senior year?

Let us not forget that one of the most practical ways to finish strong your senior year is in the books. This is something that colleges pay special attention to when reviewing applications and transcripts. Do you want to be one of the one-third of college freshmen who have to take remedial courses in college just because you slacked off your senior year? According to Dr. Hansen of Quintessential Careers, here are a couple of academic tidbits to keep in mind when senioritis rears its ugly head:

1. Colleges often request first and second semester grades even after admittance letters have been sent. They do have the right to document and inquire about any grade slip.

2. Some selective colleges even "downgrade" your application when they notice a severe drop in rigor of class choices on your senior year schedule.

3. Worst case scenario: you took it so easy that you fell one credit short of graduating high school with all your buddies. It's personally embarrassing and not impressive to any college.[10]

When it comes to relationships, senioritis can become a different kind of issue. The friends who have stood by you during thick and thin so far, most likely won't be going to your college with you. If you are dating someone, there is the big decision coming up as to whether or not you will try to make the relationship work long distance. With family, you have to emotionally prepare for not having them around each day to hear the best thing and worst thing that happened to you that day. The tension created in all these situations can leave room for you to head off to college with burned bridges and bad feelings. Pray about each of these situations as they arise, and ask God to guide you in His will for which friendships to maintain, His wisdom in whether or not to break up with your boyfriend, and His patience in dealing with family members who are possibly more emotional than you are about your leaving.

Emily Wilkinson, a high school youth program director at a church in Dallas, spends the last five weeks of her students' senior ministry preparing girls for what to expect in college. Even in this special time with her senior girls, the first lesson is "Before you get to college, you first have to finish high school." Emily speaks to her girls about ending well with a good reputation, a solid academic standing, and leaving relationships that are on good terms. When emphasizing the importance of leaving with a good name, she reminds her students of Proverbs 22:1, which states that "A good name is more desirable than riches; to be esteemed is better than silver or gold." Reality is that the people in your life your senior year (teachers, friends, boyfriends, neighbors) don't go away. You *will* see them again in restaurants, at the grocery store, and in the malls when you come home for weekend and holiday visits. Do you really want to dread coming home because you will have to spend your time avoiding so many people? End the tension now, and leave with a clean slate for your own sake. Plus, these are the very people that write your college, sorority, and possibly even job recommendations down the road. It really is important to continue to live above reproach even in those last days that you think don't count. Yes, this means you really do have to finish writing all those graduation-thank you notes!

Gresham is a great example of ending with a good reputation. Early in her schooling years, Gresham's parents decided to send all four children in her family to a newly forming private Christian school. Sometimes frustrated with that decision to move from a high-profile, big public high school system with a state championship, winning football team to a budding new private Christian school, Gresham stayed obedient to her parents and decided to finish high school there. Her high school class of twenty-one would be the largest high school class thus far to graduate from this unique private school setting. Naturally, in a class this small, everybody knows everybody's business—for better or worse. As this class approached its senior year, not everyone was getting along, and several classmates were making decisions contrary to the will of God for their lives. In an attempt to refocus for their senior year, Gresham and a few of her friends organized a class trip together before the school year began. Although many thought this to be a cheesy idea, God ordained for every member of the senior class to be present at that retreat. Thanks to Gresham's obedience and the leadership of a godly teacher who served as chaperone and discussion facilitator, God opened door after door for brokenness, healing, and restoration during the course of those few days. Friendships were restored, addictions were confessed and broken, and a spirit of servanthood and leadership overwhelmed the hearts of each senior. They made a decision during that special weekend to be examples to the many fellow schoolmates following close behind of how to live out loud the Christian walk. They wanted to leave a legacy behind that would start a tradition—"**Seniors here live boldly for the Lord, serve one another, and love each other.**" Talk about finishing strong! The example that Gresham and her classmates set will no doubt be setting the standard for future generations.

What kind of legacy are you and your senior class leaving for future generations?

Senioritis should not become a chronic issue because Colossians 3:17 states, "And whatever you do, whether in word or deed, do it all in the name of the Lord Jesus, giving thanks to God the Father through him." It's easy to fall short of your goals at the very end when you are so eager to just be done with it and move on. I think that feeling of having one foot still in high school and the other in college is magnified when college application deadlines are due, local sorority informational meetings start up, and your attention is divided between where you are and where you are going. Even though this book is designed to help you begin to prepare for this next phase, I also encourage you to make the most of this pivotal, powerful, and most influential time of your high school career. It is, after all, the only high school senior year you will have.

Chapter Two Reflection Questions

1. What are ways you are ending your senior year of high school well?

2. What kind of reputation are you leaving behind?

3. Are you prepared to leave who you were in high school and allow God to change and mold you for the better during the next few years?

Digging Deeper

■ Ending well in high school your senior year makes for a smoother transition into college. What are things you can be working on now in these four areas to ensure you finish strong?

- Academic finish–1 Corinthians 9:24
  Practical examples:

- Physical finish–Colossians 3:23
  Practical examples:

- Spiritual finish–Acts 20:24
  Practical examples:

- Relational finish–Hebrews 12:14
  Practical examples:

- ■ Why is ending with a good name (or reputation) important?

  - Ecclesiastes 7:1

  - Proverbs 22:1-2

  - Proverbs 3:3-4

PART ONE
GROWING IN
THE ACADEMIC LIFE

And Jesus grew in *wisdom* and stature, and in favor with God and men.
—Luke 2:52

Proverbs 2:2 says, "turning your ear to wisdom and applying your heart to understanding" will lead us to victorious lives. God created us with curious minds and He delights when we seek to know truth. College lectures, textbooks, and various curricula will introduce you to and inform you about the way our world works from the perspectives of history, politics, mathematics, sociology, technology, human sexuality, and hundreds of other courses found in a college course catalog. Maintaining a Christian worldview during all of your class experiences will allow you to see the world through God's lens.

In his remarkable book, *How To Stay Christian in College*, J. Budziszewski, a professor himself, challenges Christian students to practice discernment in each college class. He said, "Discernment is a Christian intellectual virtue. A virtue is a trait you should have like love, courage, gentleness, and faithfulness. An 'intellectual' virtue is a virtue of the mind, like wisdom."[11] So, as you seek knowledge and wisdom, stay wise by seeking ultimate truth in the Word of God.

During your college career, Satan will have a creative way of making the origin of man and nature and human sexuality appear very logical and alluring. Don't let your "wisdom leg" get wobbly just because your professor has a convincing Darwinist argument. God's Word is truth and has stood the test of time.

Honoring the Lord by giving Him your very best academically is key to your success in college. You may be tested over things you don't agree with—that's sometimes how it goes. Ultimate wisdom is found in Him alone, not by professors, theories, or the most current research. Stay true to your Lord by keeping an eternal perspective and your priorities in order...and you will be off to a great start.

Chapter 3

FIRST THINGS FIRST-WHY ARE YOU GOING TO COLLEGE?

> Now we ask you, brothers, to respect those who work hard among you, who are over you in the Lord and who admonish you.
>
> —1 Thessalonians 5:12

Has anyone ever asked you that question point blank? What is your true motivation in wanting to go to college? If you are having trouble answering this question, Katharine Hansen writes in her article "What Good is a College Education Anyway?" five ways college can make you a better person:

1. It will likely make you more prosperous.
2. It will give you a better quality of life.
3. It will give you the power to change the world.

4. It will be something you can pass on to your children.
5. It makes you a major contributor to the greatest nation on earth.[12]

Hansen makes a sound case. In 2006, The U.S. Census Bureau released a statement revealing estimated average earnings for adults twenty-five or older by education.

Illustration 1

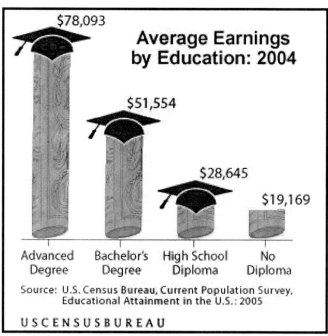

Those with advanced degrees had average annual earnings of $78,093; those with bachelor's degrees made an average of $51, 554; those with a high school diploma earned an average of $28,645; and those with no diploma averaged $19,169 as annual income.[13] It comes as no surprise that a college degree does indeed give you the potential to make a fine living.

Perhaps fulfilling a dream is the reason you are attending college. Maybe it's because it's an expectation set by family tradition. It could even be that you enjoy learning and this is the logical next step in your education. Or you might just want a chance to explore life, meet new people, and show some independence. In *God's Invitation: A Challenge to College Students*, Henry Blackaby presents the clearest reason why Christians should go to college: "A university education is not the end but the beginning. The education you obtain is merely a tool God gives you so you can be more effective in His assignment for you. The question at the end of life will not be: 'What degree did you earn?' But, 'What did you DO with your education? What did you invest your life in?"[14] That is a powerful perspective to have when you enter the door of your first college class.

Whatever the reason, know that this experience does not come easily or cheaply. Another statistic from the U.S. Census Bureau found that in 2003 only 27 percent of adults over the age of twenty-five had a college degree.[15] Although numbers are higher than in years past, the opportunity to attend university is still far from being enjoyed by all. Be wary of taking "lightly" the fact that you have this opportunity. Not everyone has the opportunity, and this is mainly due to cost. *At the turn of the century, average annual tuition, books, and room and board costs for a year of college in this country was greater than $10,000 per year per student, and costs have been steadily rising ever since.*[16] That means, on average, a four-year college experience could potentially cost at minimum $40,000. That's quite a chunk of change!

Secretary of Education Margaret Spellings admits, "We know higher education is the key to our children's future and the American Dream, yet it is becoming more unaffordable and less attainable."[17] If you want the college experience, and this undeniably high cost is preventing you from going, then rest assured that more scholarships than most people are aware of are out there waiting for the taking. During your senior year, and even after, it is worth the time to make special efforts to find out about scholarship opportunities and financial aid through your high school, school district, community, and the university you are planning to attend. Consider these Web sites and lists of nationally known scholarship opportunities to help soften the financial burden of college expenses:

- www.FASFA.us
- www.collegeview.com/financialaid/index. html
- www.collegeboard.com
- www.finaid.org
- www.savingforcollege.com[18]

If you are already engaged in the college experience or if you are about to enter the world of university life, then somebody (maybe even you) is paying for it. With that, a genuine respect should be paid to the person who is financially allowing you to experience this great opportunity. If you have the privilege of attending a college or university, then please recognize that the Lord has opened a great door for you. The person who is financially supporting this endeavor (even if you work to pay your way through college) deserves your best academically.

Every college campus will offer an array of activities going on 24/7 that will be more attractive than going to class or studying for a test. A never-ending list of cool people will come into your life whom you will want to spend time with. And, without mom and dad there to guide you along the way, who's to tell you what to do and when? There are endless adventures to be had, people to meet, and memories to make, but the worst adventure or memory would be packing up after a semester because you blew it.

Take the first step toward pursuing wisdom by respecting the opportunity now before you. Honor God, your family, and those supporting you through this college experience with your very best. With that mindset, you will be ready for the ride of your life—guilt free!

Chapter Three Reflection Questions

1. Have you thanked the person financially responsible for your opportunity to go to college either in person or by a handwritten letter?

2. Take the time to total the average cost of a year, then four years at your potential university. What did you discover?

3. What are ways that you have researched and pursued scholarship opportunities?

4. Name the people God has blessed you with who will be your support system you can call on as you transition into this new world of college.

Digging Deeper

■ What does the Bible say about wisdom?

- Proverbs 2:1-8 paraphrase _____
- Psalm 110:10 paraphrase_____
- James 1:5-6 paraphrase_____

■ How is wisdom most overtly handed down to you in college?

- How can you determine what is worldly theory and what is Truth?

  - Colossians 2:6-8
  - 1 Timothy 4:7
  - Hebrews 13:8

- What should our attitude be towards professors who provoke lively discussion on controversial topics and who test you on concepts with which you don't necessarily agree?

  - 1 Peter 2:17

- How should you handle the opportunity to go to college, especially in light of the cost?

  - Luke 16:10
  - Luke 19:17
  - Matthew 25:21

- Why should you apply for scholarships?

  - 1 Thessalonians 5:12
  - Deuteronomy 5:16

- Have you written that thank-you note yet?

Chapter 4

THE SCHEDULE…
MAKING IT WORK
FOR YOU

There is a time for everything, and a season for
every activity under heaven.
                                      —Ecclesiastes 3:1

If college is the time when you are supposed to
grow in wisdom by taking all these intellectually
stimulating classes, how can you make the most of
that time if you're not in school from a solid 8:00 A.M.
to 3:30 P.M. like you were in high school? This is a
very tricky part of college life that takes awhile to get
used to. Up until now, you have lived by a bell. You
get up early, try to grab a bite to eat, catch a ride, and
get to school on time because you don't want that
third tardy. And, when you are nodding off in fifth
period due to the after lunch low-blood-sugar-lull,
you make the call to stay at school either because

your crush sits behind you in sixth period class…
or because you can't cheer that night if you're not
at school a full day.

Obviously, college is different. You set your
own schedule, and it's called "hours." Here's how it
works. A college class for one semester is typically
"three" hours. This means you will attend this class
three hours a week. Let's pretend it is scheduled for
Monday, Wednesday, and Friday from 10:00 to 11:00
A.M. Another class that is three hours may meet on

Illustration 2

Sample College Schedule: 15 Hours of Class				
	Monday	Tuesday	Wednesday	Thursday	Friday
8:00	History 106		History 106		History 106
9:00		Political Science 106		Political Science 106	
10:00	Math 365		Math 365		Math 365
11:00					
12:00					
1:00					
2:00	English Lit 204		English Lit 204		English Lit 204
3:00					
4:00		Geography 101		Geography 101	
5:00					
6:00	Sorority Meetings				
7:00		Bible Study			
8:00				Intramural Soccer Games	

Tuesdays and Thursdays from 1:30 to 3:00 P.M. You
may only attend that class twice a week, but you are
still receiving three hours of instruction.

Most college students average about fifteen hours per semester (which means they are enrolled in five classes that meet for three hours each per week). Some college classes are just two hours (such as kinesiology or leadership classes), and some science labs may be up to four hours. Regardless, the number of hours simply represents the amount of lecture or lab time you have to actually attend during the week.

This sounds easy, right? Once you get the lingo down, that part *is* easy. You may also be thinking, I'm in school between thirty and thirty-five hours a week now…college should be a breeze with only fifteen! For some people, it is. For most, that mentality gets them in a bit of trouble, and here's why.

For every college "hour" attended in lecture, most college Web sites recommend that between two and three hours should be applied in reading, completing assignments, or studying. So if you are taking twelve hours of lecture time in one semester, that means you will need to allow up to three times (between twenty-four and thirty-six hours per week) as much in preparation time to be successful in those classes. Still sound easy? Great!

The hard part for my friends and me in college was being disciplined enough to make that study and preparation time when there was so much other "more fun" stuff going on all around us, all the time.

With that said, setting up your first college schedule your first semester can be quite a daunting task. Most orientation sessions will help you figure out what classes you need according to your degree plan. Mary Ann Newbill, a college admissions counselor for *My Footpath,* gives five critical components to consider when setting up your first college schedule:

1. Consider time day when you would most want to be in class and be able to focus in class.
2. Consider college requirements and number of hours required for you to be considered a full-time student.
3. Consider the types of courses you can handle in one semester. Look at prerequisites needed for future classes. Also consider a balance of subjects you might enjoy versus subjects that might bring challenge. If you are not great in math, don't load up on math-related courses in one semester.
4. Consider the campus size and classroom location. If you will be attending a large campus, make sure you have given yourself enough time between back-to-back classes.
5. Consider placement test results. As mentioned earlier, passing AP exams usually satisfies certain basic requirements. However, some colleges require you to take placement tests to identify which basic level courses in which to place you your freshman year.[19]

May I make one more suggestion here? Even if you know without a shadow of a doubt you want to be a biomedical science major because you aspire to become a medical doctor, please just take the general requirements your freshman and sophomore years instead of trying to jump ahead. If you happen to change your mind and want to switch to business later on, it won't be nearly as traumatic!

To back up a little, let's talk about general requirements. These are the classes that the university requires every student to take in order to have a well-rounded education and be eligible for graduation in years to come.

For example, most students have to take a series of math, English, history, science, kinesiology, and arts classes as a "core curriculum" before entering into the "specific major" classes. This is similar to the core classes you were required to take in high school. It usually takes about four semesters, or two years, to complete all these requirements. If you have taken AP courses in high school and are one of the 917,051 high school students who received college credit from high AP test scores[20], more than likely they will be applied to these classes. Kudos to you if you have earned early college credit this way! These general classes that everyone is forced to take are usually held in lecture halls that hold three hundred people and are some of the toughest classes (some call it the weeding out process) in the university system. Finishing those up first will give you more flexibility if you decide to change your major down the road.

31

In any event, be prepared to spend a lot less physical class time in college than you are currently used to and lots more study time in the library or in your dorm. This means setting a schedule of classes with times when you are fresh and ready to learn and also gives you plenty of study time during those down hours in the day. For me, I slept in every chance I had, so 8:00 A.M. and morning classes were ideal for me. This early schedule forced me out of bed, kept me from itching to be anywhere else during class (except in my bed), and allowed me to be finished with classes by the time early afternoon rolled around. This meant I could spend the rest of the day on campus studying or reading (which I confess did not always happen).

My husband, on the other hand, was an early bird and loved to study and read in the mornings. He would read and prepare early, attend some late morning and early afternoon classes, and spend a chunk of the late afternoon studying and reading as well.

You know yourself better than anyone, so try to arrange your classes in a way that will maximize your time. One great piece of advice given to me was to think of college like an eight-to-five job. From eight o'clock in the morning to five o'clock in the afternoon, you are either in class or studying; this way you have your nights free (study-free, that is). I confess this didn't always work for me, but neither did studying at night when all my friends were having dinner together at my favorite restaurant and hanging out.

One more thing about your first college schedule. Once you get your classes set and figure out the best times and places to study, don't forget to schedule in some rest amidst all your academic and social activities. I know too many people who have gotten extremely ill during their first year of college because they wore themselves out trying to do everything college has to offer in the first semester. Pulling "all-nighter" study sessions without proper sleep makes you vulnerable to all kinds of illnesses—which take all the fun out of college.

By scheduling your classes in a time frame that fits you and your mental alertness best, you will be able to maximize your class and study time in a way that will keep you from procrastinating, which is a college student's worst habit! I'll end this chapter with a great passage by Charles Colson as he describes how we, as Christians, should prioritize our time and schedule:

> There are at least four applications for this biblical view of time: First, we should honor our bodies by keeping sensible schedules and getting the rest we need. We have enough time to work [for you, study], rest, love our families and friends, worship, and exercise. Second, we must build into our schedules prayer and meditation on God's Word. Keeping God and his Word at the forefront of our minds helps us develop the biblical notion of time. Third, we can say no. Our overscheduled lives are testimony that our notion of time has not been formed by a biblical

worldview. Finally, we can enjoy the freedom of the Sabbath, that foretaste of our eternal rest with God.[21]

Chapter Four Reflection Questions

1. Are you an early riser or a night owl?

2. What would be the best time of day for you to be able to focus in class? When would you be able to focus best when studying?

3. When is orientation week at your college or university? Are you registered for this?

4. Have you prayed that God would prepare the perfect schedule for you during that crucial first semester?

Digging Deeper

■ What does the Bible say about managing time?

- Ecclesiastes 3:1
- 2 Timothy 3:14-16
- Proverbs 20:13 (huge college trap!)

Chapter 5

* *

WHAT'S YOUR MAJOR?

"For I know the plans I have for you," declares
the Lord, "plans to prosper you and not to harm
you, plans to give you hope and a future."
—Jeremiah 29:11

The joke in any college setting is that when
a group of students is together meeting one
another for the first time, the most common
question is always, "So, what's your major?" And
why shouldn't it be? It's common to all students and
should be a safe question, right?

Choosing a major is definitely a huge decision,
and the process is different for everyone. Some folks
are born with a passion to be something that never
changes their whole life, and that is fantastic. The
rest of us sit and wonder again and again, *What will I
be when I grow up?* I still ask that question of myself

now! Obviously, the first step in any decision of this magnitude requires prayer. Lift up to the Lord your desire to follow Him, and ask for His guidance in what He would want you to be pursuing. Even with prayer, deciding on a major can be a stressful decision. Should you go with something you love, something you know will provide great job security, or something that you're simply curious about? All these questions factor in as you make that decision. In her book *Getting Ready for College*, Polly Berent shoots it straight to students: "Many would agree that you might as well choose a major you can enjoy. Why? The job market is changing rapidly. By the time you graduate, the unpredictable economy might be in the best or worst of times. Plus, studies indicate that adults should now figure on having four to six different careers in their lifetime."[22] Thank goodness you don't have to decide your freshman year! The authors of *College Survival 7th Edition* encourage students to wait a year or two before declaring a major—most advisors discourage it. "You need to answer many questions before choosing a major. What kind of job are you planning on? Do you wish to attend graduate school? And of course, what interests you? These questions can be answered after your freshman year, after you have decided what you like, and after you have figured out the subjects in which you excel."[23]

So the pressure is off…for now. Don't feel like you have to figure out what you will do with the rest of your life during your college orientation. If you have given your life to Christ, and by consistently pursuing Him and becoming aware of the gifts and talents He has given you, direction will eventually come. It might not happen your freshman year, but I can promise God has great things in store for you.

Now, for those of you who are itching to get a little more concrete direction in choosing a major, here are some helpful and practical things to consider. What are your interests? What are your skills? What were your favorite high school courses? What do you find comes easily to you but is difficult for others?[24] These are just a few of the questions found in Laurence Shatkin's book called the *90 Minute College Major Matcher*, a very helpful overview of the wide ranges of college majors with matching careers out there from which to choose.

What happens if you think you are good at something, then find out halfway through college that you're not? Or that you don't like it anymore? Let me ease the tension for you now. YOU CAN ALWAYS CHANGE YOUR MAJOR! That is why I encourage college students to take the general classes required by the university (regardless of your major) first in case there is a change within those first two years…then no hours are lost. Unfortunately, I didn't follow my own advice, and I got myself in a bit of a pickle.

I had always struggled between becoming a teacher or a journalist. Both seemed like paths that were right for me, but I just wasn't sure. During my first orientation meeting, I distinctly remember being given a card with information from my original college application. The speaker during that session asked us to review the information on the card and make any changes if necessary. My card read that I had declared early education as my major, but something in me really wanted to be a broadcast journalist—that day. I glanced at my mom, looking for that nod of approval, and then crossed out what was written and changed my major the first day of orientation. This wouldn't have been such a bad thing if I had stuck to my own advice and taken only general core classes my first two years. No. I wanted to dive right into those journalism classes, so off I went. The beginning of my junior year...you guessed it, I changed my major back to education. The only problem was that fifteen of my hours dedicated solely to journalism did not count on the education track. So my parents were out that money (a whole semester's worth of classes), and I had to make up all that lost time in the education department. I think you see the logic that I missed.

The good news is that it's not that hard to change if you get to that point. All it takes is a meeting with your advisor (whom you will most likely meet at your orientation) and supportive parents. An advisor can be a great sounding board for you, not only if you are thinking of changing your major, but also if you are struggling with certain classes or professors. Advisors usually have a good handle on the faculty personalities, the difficulty of classes, and an overall perspective of what it takes to make it in that field of study. It's a good idea to make an appointment each year—if not once a semester—with your advisor to touch base and talk over how things are going academically for you. Advisors usually enjoy getting to know students on a regular basis and want you to be happy and successful during your college years.

I wish I could offer more advice on how to actually pick a major. If there is something you know deep inside you without a doubt that you feel called to pursue, by all means declare it. But, if you are wishy-washy and a little nervous about the whole college thing in general, don't hesitate to declare "general studies" or something similar as a major. Eventually, you will have to get more specific, but it takes some college students actual college time to figure out what that is. My grandmother always used to say that figuring out what you *don't* want in life is just as important as figuring out what you *do* want.

At the end of the day think of your career path in these terms: "Education must be oriented to preparation for a calling and not just training for a career."[25] Thankfully, the Lord knows exactly the calling He has placed in your life, and as long as you seek Him, you can't make a bad decision.

Chapter Five Reflection Questions

1. Have you begun to pray about the major you should select in college?

2. What are things you think you have done best, done well, and done average in your life?

3. What are gifts God has given you that you sense will play a role in a vocation down the road?

4. List three people in your life you could talk to or bounce ideas off who would be wise in helping you determine a major.

Digging Deeper

■ Big picture: What does the Bible say about God's will for our lives?

- Ecclesiastes 12:13 _____ God
- Matthew 22:34-40 _____ God
- Jeremiah 29:11 _____God
- Proverbs 16:3 _____ God
- Psalm 32:8 and Isaiah 58:11 _____ God
- Philippians 1:6_____ God

■ Smaller picture: How do I do the above to figure out what college I should go to and what I should major in?

- _____ Him that He has a plan.
  - Proverbs 3:5-6
  - Psalm 33:11
  - Proverbs 19:21
- _____ Him first, others next.
  - Matthew 6:33-34
  - Proverbs 20:18
  - Proverbs 15:22
- _____ Him to show you what His will is.
  - Matthew 7:7-8
  - Psalm 25:4-5
- _____ to Him continually.
  - 1 Thessalonians 5:16

Big picture answers: Fear God, Love God, Trust God, Commit to God, Lean on God, Believe God.

Smaller picture answers: Trust Him, Seek Him, Ask Him, Pray to Him.

Chapter 6

STUDY TIPS AND TRICKS

And whatever you do, whether in word or deed,
do it all in the name of the Lord Jesus, giving
thanks to God the Father through Him.
—Colossians 3:17

Colby is an all-American catch. He's tall,
handsome, driven, loves God, and is the life
of any party. His first semester at Texas Tech
University he made a 4.0. This is what Colby had
to say about surviving and succeeding that first
semester:

As far as classes go, probably the most important
thing was just doing things in a timely manner.
Of course, don't procrastinate. A lot of people
would come home from classes and either go
to sleep or just hang out and party. When I got

43

home from classes, I usually would sit down for a little while and check my e-mail or catch a fifteen-minute cat nap. But after that, I would make sure all my work was done for the day before going to do anything else. So many people would still be up at midnight or later working on things when I was already done with everything and having a good time. By making sure I finished all my work in the afternoon or early evening, I had the entire night to have fun when other people would still be slaving away. Also, plenty of people in college just skip class whenever they feel like it. That's like throwing money away and you'll get so far behind. You just have to get up and go no matter how tired you are or what you did last night. I introduced myself to my professors on the first day of class, which gives you a better chance of them remembering you and helping you out. Not waiting to do assignments that are due in the future makes a big difference. Also, it goes without saying that you need to be studying in a place where you won't be distracted easily. Mainly a lot of college is just a big test of self-control. Of course, the best thing you can do is just pray about it. Talking to Him can never hurt. Ask Him to give you the strength, patience, discipline, etc. to do what is needed.

Well, there you go. This chapter could end here. Colby has the right attitude in approaching his studies by wanting to honor the Lord through his work and trusting that God will give him what he needs to persevere. And on top of that, he gives it his best by showing up, not procrastinating, and by being proactive about meeting professors and time management. His approach is similar to the advice Cal Newport gives in his book titled *How to Win at College*. Cal puts it this way, "Being a college student is a lot like being a professional golfer… you should do some amount of school work every single day."[26]

My parents gave me some similar simple advice: Just show up to class, do your homework, and study for your tests. This simplistic wisdom is so true. Giving college your academic best simply means showing up and following through.

The part about showing up to class doesn't sound that hard until that Friday afternoon class always gets in the way of your weekend road trip or that Monday morning eight o'clock class comes a little too early after a weekend of fun. Anyway you look at it, your professors will be on your team if you at least make the effort to show up and participate. In some classes, the professor will even take attendance. The discussions in class are usually lectures of important highlights needed for later, so learn how to take good notes—and show up!

The second part of that sage old advice still applies today. College classes and grading systems are not like high school, where homework and projects count for the majority of your grade and major tests count for a small percentage. Usually, it is just the opposite. Most of your grade for a course will depend on one or a few exams throughout the semester. With that said, doing "weekly homework" of keeping up with the reading is very important. If you're trying to take notes on a lecture that you have no background knowledge about because you haven't read the assigned chapters for that session, you will be lost—during class…and later. And, if by chance, in a math course or something similar there is official written homework–do it. Most college professors don't assign homework for the sake of a daily grade; they mean business. This concept may be trivial to those of you who were valedictorian, top ten percent of your class, or never had to study to get through high school, but heed the warning that college is not like high school!

The final piece of advice from my parents still stands as well. Study. Not like in high school, cramming in the cafeteria before school or during lunch for a quiz that afternoon. Study—as in many sessions of preparations, making note cards or talking out lecture points with a study buddy. I do know that if you respect the institution and attempt those three things (show up, do the homework, and study), then you shouldn't be too worried about your grades.

So, in order to get you off on the right foot, let us recap some major points that will be a sure-fire way to keep anybody out of the doghouse, free from sorority probation, and off the hook from playing catch-up the rest of your college career.

1. Learn how to take good notes.

In the school system I taught in, one of the college strategies that was presented district-wide was the Cornell note-taking method (which most students came back praising over and over after using them in both high school and college).

Illustration 3

The Cornell Note-taking System

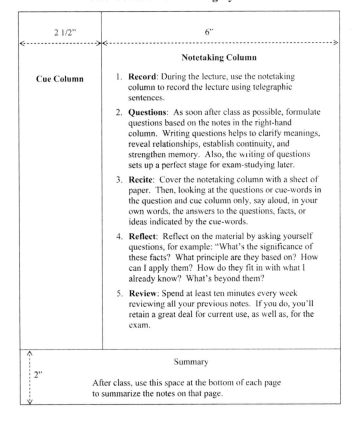

2 1/2"	6"
	Notetaking Column
Cue Column	1. **Record**: During the lecture, use the notetaking column to record the lecture using telegraphic sentences.
	2. **Questions**: As soon after class as possible, formulate questions based on the notes in the right-hand column. Writing questions helps to clarify meanings, reveal relationships, establish continuity, and strengthen memory. Also, the writing of questions sets up a perfect stage for exam-studying later.
	3. **Recite**: Cover the notetaking column with a sheet of paper. Then, looking at the questions or cue-words in the question and cue column only, say aloud, in your own words, the answers to the questions, facts, or ideas indicated by the cue-words.
	4. **Reflect**: Reflect on the material by asking yourself questions, for example: "What's the significance of these facts? What principle are they based on? How can I apply them? How do they fit in with what I already know? What's beyond them?
	5. **Review**: Spend at least ten minutes every week reviewing all your previous notes. If you do, you'll retain a great deal for current use, as well as, for the exam.
2"	Summary After class, use this space at the bottom of each page to summarize the notes on that page.

This is when the page is divided and notes are taken on one side—leaving room for study questions and terms on the other. At the end of every note-taking session, students were asked to summarize in three sentences or less the content of that day. This is also a great strategy for understanding the big picture of the content. The professor does want you to know the details discussed, but more importantly he or she wants you to have a broad understanding of the concept. With this big picture concept, many of the multiple-choice questions come test time won't stump you. If this method of note-taking isn't your favorite, then try other ways until you find what works for you.

2. Find a study buddy in each class

The first couple of classes you take, this may be awkward because you don't recognize or know anyone yet. I found that most people in the class are usually thinking the same thing, so when everyone gets up to leave that first class, grab someone around you that you think you would get along with and introduce yourself. Ask to see if he or she wants to exchange e-mail addresses or numbers to get notes in case one of you has to miss a class. Most people sit in the same place every class, so, over time, this relationship might become a study buddy! Getting together with a group of people and talking out the lectures and readings is of great value to all in the group. First, they might have gotten something in the lecture that you missed, or they might actually understand some of the reading that bogged you down. Research has proven that communicating ideas during the learning process improves the learning process as a whole.[27] You can't really do this alone, so make some friends in every class!

3. **Read assigned chapters on the syllabus before you go to class.**

This is a big deal—HUGE. I simply did not understand the big deal in reading seven chapters on a subject in a massive textbook I didn't really understand in one week *before* I heard a lecture on it. If I could go back and do my college classes all over again, this is for sure one thing I would change. Even if the chapters seem never ending or the content seems overwhelming, having background knowledge concerning the topics covered in each lecture class will greatly improve your memory retention, attention span, and note-taking during each class.

Also, getting in this habit of keeping up with the reading allows for less procrastination later. When a mid-term exam covers fourteen chapters, no hiding in a hole for a weekend playing catch-up will be necessary. Keeping on track takes a large degree of discipline, but keeps you out of trouble, for sure.

As much fun as it would be to go to the park that gorgeous Thursday afternoon when all your buds are playing Frisbee golf, FINISH the reading assigned. It will pay off, I promise.

4. **Find a secret place to study/read that is without distractions.**

Most students assume that the library is a safe place to study–NOT ALWAYS! There was one particular library on our campus...the business library (where all the beautiful boys studied) that became a social event by nine o'clock every night. Even if I had gotten there early in the afternoon to read, so many folks eventually gathered around visiting, catching up, getting numbers, that all the activity made it difficult to concentrate. Another danger zone is coffee houses. You know what a Starbuck's is like when it is jam-packed full of folks. Not a place to quietly study at all! One specific coffee shop near our campus had the cool couches, groovy atmosphere, and incredible hot chocolate, but it was THE sorority and fraternity hang-out. Once a group of guys studying saw a group of girls studying, then all "mack" was on...and no studying whatsoever took place.

Dorm rooms would seem like a good option, but those can be pretty rowdy and full of distracting activity as well. The best places are the ones where you can hide yourself away from lots of activity, but are still inviting enough to keep awake. Corridors of some buildings, student centers, and top floors of non-social libraries can provide corners of quiet and comfort that will allow time there to be wisely spent.

5. **Complete writing assignments and projects prior to the night before they are due.**

Two obvious reasons. One is procrastination—not a good thing. Pulling all-nighters can become a trendy habit on college campuses, but it's no good for anyone. Having math homework or an English assignment ready to go before the day before relieves so much pressure.

The other reason involves the wonderful world of technology. As most probably experienced in high school, last minute computer problems only arise when a project is due the next day. It is almost guaranteed that the Internet connection will miraculously shut down, the ink will run out, or the computer's hard drive will crash right in the middle of printing out a masterpiece at three o'clock in the morning right before it's due.

6. **Introduce yourself to your professors and don't be afraid to ask for help!**

If the professor knows your face (and maybe even your name), he or she is much more likely to help you be successful. Introduce yourself at the beginning of the semester and express that you are excited or interested in the course. You might even ask him if he has any particular advice for being successful. As a teacher myself, I can tell you that educators and professors appreciate when students take interest in their subject. It takes a level of maturity to do this, but the reward is great when you are teetering between a B or C at the end of the semester. If the professor knows you, has seen you come in for help, and knows you've given it your best, he might help you out. Also, most classes at large universities will hold study sessions led by teaching assistants or graduate students. Always attend these sessions and keep record of your attendance. They are there to help you, and this is another way that the professor knows you have tried. And by the way, it's extremely helpful and beneficial to begin building relationships with professors early. When you graduate, you will need letters of recommendation from college or university level employees—preferably from those who know you.

Once the semester stride starts, this will all become very natural. It's not like you've never studied before (you did get into college somehow). College just takes a little more proactive effort on your part. Staying on top of the academic end is not only a priority, it makes the other parts of college so much more enjoyable. Ask the Lord to begin preparing you for the intellectual challenge that college offers. Do your best to glorify Him in this area of your life, and everything else about college will seem to fall right into place.

Chapter Six Reflection Questions

1. What good study habits did you practice in high school?

2. What bad study habits need to be forgotten from high school?

3. What specific study habits do you think you need to acquire for university level classes?

4. Evaluate whom you are studying for. (Are you studying to please your parents, stay on the dance team, or because you don't want to let your teachers down?)

5. Pray to the Lord that He will provide the tools you need to be successful academically.

Digging Deeper

■ What does the Bible say about study habits?

- Colossians 3:23

- Colossians 3:17

PART TWO
GROWING IN
THE PHYSICAL LIFE

And Jesus grew in wisdom and *stature*, and in favor with God and men.
—Luke 2:52

Apopular exhibit that toured the nation not long ago was BodyWorlds. This surreal experience displayed actual components of our skin, organs, bones, muscles and even blood vessels through the revolutionary scientific procedure called plastination. Through this process, we now have a full body glimpse of what is really inside us. When my husband and I toured it for the first time, we kept saying to ourselves, *How could someone not believe in God after seeing this?*

Our bodies could only have been created by God Himself. Genesis 1:26-27 states "Then God said, 'Let us make man in our image, in our likeness, and let them rule over the fish of the sea and birds of the air, over the livestock, over all the earth, and over all the creatures that move along the ground.' So God created man in His own image, in the image of God he created him; male and female he created them." And for those of you who struggle with the way God made you, consider this quote by Priscilla Evans Shirer in one of my favorite books, *A Jewel in His Crown:*

> If you are like most women, you have probably looked in the mirror and wondered why in the world God decided to make you the way He did. Maybe you have always been totally dissatisfied with the way you were created, and have always wished for something "better." We are made in God's own likeness; how insulted He must feel when we do this. How dare we insult a holy God, wishing we looked different or were, in fact, different people all together? Wouldn't you be hurt if your son or daughter looked identical to you and hated every minute of it? I wonder how God must feel about us when we cry and pout about the very work of His own hands."[28]

God knows what we look like—He created us! And remember that we are not to worry about those little things that aren't perfect on the outside, for Proverbs 31:30 reminds us that "Charm is deceptive and beauty is fleeting, but a woman who fears the Lord is to be praised."

Regardless of how we or the world sees our external body, we have a responsibility to take care of it. Even at your age your body is still growing in form (or stature) and demands only a few physical requirements. Our body's basic necessities are as simple as water, food, and movement—from there it takes care of itself. On most given days, we don't really think of it that way. We just look forward to breakfast, lunch, dinner, a nice walk in the morning, and maybe that bottle of water after a hard workout. What's even more unreal than the physical workings of our body on a daily basis is the fact that, as Christians, "our bodies are members of Christ Himself" (1 Corinthians 6:15). That is why later in that same scripture, Paul calls our body a "temple of the Holy Spirit" and tells us to "honor God with your body"(1 Corinthians 6: 19-20).

So, as your physical body continues to grow and change, you are called to honor God with it. Unfortunately, there is an enemy out there who would love nothing more than for you to destroy it. Satan is the king of temptations and knows our trouble spots and weak areas when it comes to physical needs. He tries to get us to destroy our bodies with bad habits, immoral behavior, and out of balance living. Even Jesus Himself was tested and tempted by Satan. In Matthew 4:1 we read,

> Then Jesus was led by the Spirit into the desert to be tempted by the devil. After fasting forty days and forty nights, he was hungry. The tempter

came to him and said, "If you are the Son of God, tell these stones to become bread."

Unbelievable! The devil tried to tempt the Son of God. Even Jesus, who was not only fully God, but also fully man, had the very physical needs that we do. Satan tried to manipulate even Him in hopes of gaining power and control. Jesus had not eaten in forty days—you know He was hungry. But He also knew that He had to honor His Father with His body and not succumb to Satan's lies.

In college, you will face a mound of temptations—more than you ever did in high school. Your body is human. It has cravings. It has physical needs. As a Christian, we must fill those needs the way God intended instead of through the temporary shortcuts that Satan presents. Whether it be the areas of eating, exercising, drinking, drugs, or sexual temptation—Jesus understands. He was tempted, too. As overwhelming temptations arise during your college years, cling to truth. Honor God by making choices that bring glory to Him. The sin is not in the temptation, but in the reaction. Will your reaction to these temptations glorify God or give the enemy a foothold for a stronghold?

Chapter 7

THE EATING EXTREMES

> Therefore I tell you, do not worry about your life,
> what you will eat or drink; or about your body,
> what you will wear. Is not life more important
> than food, and the body more important than
> clothes?
>
> —Matthew 6:25

In our culture, body image is one of the most prevalent issues that Satan has perverted and distorted. The media screams that weighing eighty pounds will bring you acceptance, success, and a cover spread in the hottest magazines. Nothing could be further from the truth. Body image has become such a widespread national issue that well-known businesses and high profile figures are trying to raise awareness and send better messages to young women. I applaud Dove's corporate campaign for real beauty through the groundbreaking advertisements that use real-size women as models. I commend Maria Shriver for her vision in creating a women's conference dedicated to empowering women of all shapes and sizes. And I even appreciate former model and TV personality Tyra Banks for hosting her T-Zone camps that try to increase the self-esteem of young girls. But the truth is that self-esteem can't really change without the transforming power of God.

Psalm 139 tells us that God Himself knows when you sit, when you rise, and all your thoughts before you even have them. It also states that He knit you in your mother's womb, created your innermost being, and all your days are ordained by Him. My favorite part of this passage found in verse fourteen urges us to know we are fearfully and wonderfully made. God knows exactly what you look like and how you feel! Even knowing this, it is easy to obsess over what we look like and how we are viewed by other people. If we aren't careful, our thoughts are consumed and our habits are dictated according to the way models and movie stars look after hours of digital touchups and airbrushing.

The way you view yourself and treat your body now will be tested to the max during your college years. A study completed ten years ago by Exeter University that included 37,500 young women between the ages of twelve and fifteen revealed that over half (57.5 percent) listed appearance as the biggest concern of their lives.[29] That's not a surprising statistic when the models we compare ourselves with in the magazines are thinner than 98 percent of American women.[30] There is nothing wrong or bad about wanting to look and feel your best; the danger starts when we resort to extreme eating (or not eating) habits to attain unreasonable results for our individual body type and lifestyle. I can't think of a better time than college to start developing some *good* habits that promote healthy and balanced living.

In hopes of maintaining a healthy body the way God created us, there seem to be two major themes in all the health books: eating and exercising. This chapter will primarily focus on the eating part—what God says about it and how we can carry those ideas with us into that first college dorm. Although they go hand in hand, we will focus on the exercising element in the next chapter.

What the Bible Says about Food

Let's talk about food, specifically, what the Bible says about it. Simply put, Jesus tells us in Matthew 6:25, "Therefore I tell you, do not worry about your life, what you will eat or drink; or about your body, what you will wear. Is not life more important than food, and the body more important than clothes?" In the law of the Old Testament, God had given His people strict dietary laws about what they could and could not eat for holiness reasons. When Jesus came to fulfill the law, we became free of all those rules.

God is now more concerned about the spiritual food we put in our bodies than any fruit, vegetable, or dairy product.

However, there are great lessons for us to learn from the Old Testament days. In her inspirational book *Weigh-Down Diet,* Gwen Shamblin dissects the scriptures dealing with food and reveals some startling information. In one section, she emphasizes that God is not so much concerned about *what* we eat anymore as much as He is concerned with the *amount* that we eat. She takes her readers through the journey of the Israelites in Exodus who are being freed from the four hundred plus years of slavery under Pharaoh. Throughout their long forty-year journey led by Moses to the Promised Land, they were provided with exactly what they needed for survival[31]. In Exodus 16:1-5, 20, the scripture states:

> The whole Israelite community set out from Elim and came to the Desert of Sin, which is between Elim and Sinai, on the fifteenth day of the second month after they had come out of Egypt. In the desert the whole community grumbled against Moses and Aaron. The Israelites said to them, "If only we had died by the Lord's hand in Egypt! There we sat around pots of meat and ate all the food we wanted, but you have brought us out into this desert to starve this entire assembly to death." Then the Lord said to Moses, "I will rain down bread from heaven for you. The people are to go out each day and gather enough for that

day. In this way, I will test them and see whether they will follow my instructions. On the sixth day they are to prepare what they bring in, and this is to be twice as much as they gather on the other days." However, some of them paid no attention to Moses; they kept part of it until morning, but it was full of maggots and began to smell. So Moses was angry with them.

To use Shamblin's words, "Food was made to be a tool to serve mankind, not for man to be a slave to food."[31] **The Lord taught the Israelites to completely trust Him to provide exactly what they needed.**

Later in her book, she reveals that what took the Israelites forty years should have really only taken two weeks. The physical journey was only 180 miles from the Red Sea to the Promised Land. Unfortunately, like all of us, they tried to do things their own way and not God's. In our culture, doing things our "own way" can include eating everything in sight hoping diet pills, laxatives, and enemas can keep us from gaining the weight. Or we obsess over every little calorie and fat gram until we begin to worship food instead of God. One way or another, God will get our attention—whether it takes two weeks or forty years!

The First Extreme: Too Much

Have you ever heard the phrase "the freshman fifteen"? This common college phrase refers to the so-called fifteen pounds the average freshman gains. A *USA Today* article published in October 2006 revealed that the average weight gained for freshmen at Purdue University actually totaled 7.8 pounds for both men and women, mainly in the first semester.[32] Okay, so it's not quite the "freshman fifteen" that rolls off the tongue so much better than the "freshman 7.8," but it's still a significant weight gain for first-year college students. This happens—accidentally—for a variety of reasons: late night studying and snacking, pizza, constantly eating out, more pizza, road-trip snack stops, Coke binges for caffeine kicks, and even more pizza—just to name a few. I have to confess, I am guilty of carelessly gaining those few pounds myself during those college years. It is a horrible feeling when it hits you what you have done to yourself. Most girls who are highly active in sports, dance, or cheerleading during their junior high and high school years aren't as involved in such rigorous physical activities in college. The combination of less activity and unhealthy eating can be a dangerous combination.

The Second Extreme: Too Little

Then, of course, there is the other extreme of not eating. So many girls want to be sickly thin like the models and movie stars splattered across the entertainment magazines in the grocery aisles. College seems like the perfect place to starve themselves—mom and dad certainly aren't watching. Here are some astounding statistics about the growing popularity of eating disorders such as bulimia and anorexia:

- 5 to 10 percent of American women today are living with some form of eating disorder.
- 4 percent of college-age women have bulimia.
- Anorexia and bulimia primarily affect people in their teens and twenties.
- 1 percent of U.S. women have a binge eating disorder.
- Without treatment, up to 20 percent of people with serious eating disorders die.
- With treatment, about 60 percent of people with eating disorders recover.
- Three out of every hundred women in this country eat in a way that warrants treatment[33].

Starving yourself and depriving your body of necessary nutrients are not God's plan for your life—ever. If you are struggling in this area, I encourage you to get professional help through a counselor, dietitian, or nutritionist. This is a battle you cannot fight alone, and the earlier you get intervention, the better.

I can't move on without addressing what would be considered a "gray area" for teens called dieting. I interviewed a Christian dietitian named Stephanie Rushing who specializes in helping girls struggling with the eating disorders mentioned above. She said that dieting is the leading cause of obesity and eating disorders—the "gateway drug," so to speak. And ironically, her statistics showed that in general, the higher level of socioeconomic status of someone, the less knowledge she has of general nutrition. Dieting, which seems neutral in tone, can be very dangerous and lead to terrible things. To help girls have a more biblical perspective during her one-on-one sessions, Stephanie often uses Scripture to address tough subjects. Here are samples of a few:

- Matthew 6:24-25: "No one can serve two masters. Either he will hate the one and love the other, or he will be devoted to the one and despise the other." Her question: What is your master—food or God?
- Mark 7:18-23: "'Don't you see that nothing that enters a man from the outside can make him 'unclean'? For it doesn't go into his heart but into his stomach, then out of his body.... What comes out of a man is what makes him 'unclean'. From within, out of men's hearts, come evil thoughts, sexual immorality, theft, murder, adultery, greed, malice, deceit, lewdness, envy, slander, arrogance, and folly. All of these evils come from inside and make a man 'unclean.'" Her question: If food itself isn't the real enemy, then what is the emotional root that is causing such problems with eating?

- 1 Timothy 4:4-7: "For everything God created is good…. Have nothing to do with godless myths and old wives tales; rather train yourself to be godly." Her question: If God created food, then how can it be bad? She explains to the girls she works with that diet pills and fake supplements are quick fixes equal to "godless myths and old wives' tales," and to not be trapped by their alluring power.

These are just a few of the in-depth examples from Scripture she uses in her sessions with clients to bring to light the real issues. Stephanie takes great pride in her work and considers it an honor to be able to use the Bible to help free young women from the stronghold of lies Satan would have them believe. I am thankful that Christian dietitians like Stephanie are out there and can help us with the practicality of eating properly instead of dieting, while explaining the eternal significance these sensitive topics can have in our lives.

So you've seen both extremes of how eating can be done your own way instead of God's way—letting yourself go and letting yourself waste away. Neither is healthy or God's plan for your life. What are the best eating choices to make those first years away from home where breakfast, lunch, and dinner aren't prepared for you by mom anymore?

What the Experts Say about Overall Nutrition

I recently had the opportunity to visit the Hilton Head Health Institute (H3I) and cooking school in South Carolina for a full seven days. The things I learned in that short week are major pieces of knowledge for everyday living that I wish I had learned in high school—simple things like proper nutrition and exercise really do affect our everyday lives—especially when we are out of balance.

According to H3I, every person's body needs a certain amount of calories to sustain life. For each person that number is different. For girls, that number can be anywhere from 1,400-2,400 calories a day. The number of calories you need per day varies greatly according to your age and activity level. I encourage you to discover your metabolism (or resting metabolic rate) to help you attain a healthy amount of calories each day. Then I would start educating yourself on how many calories are in the foods you eat. In general terms, fruits and vegetables have fewer calories than potato chips and French fries. By being aware of what you eat, you will build a lifestyle that allows you to eat freely.

For example, my aunt is around fifty years old. She looks great and is very active. Many people want to know how she stays so healthy. Her answer is simple: she is aware of what she eats. She did not say obsessed, she said aware, and there is a big difference. She has learned that five small meals three to four hours apart keep her metabolism and energy levels high. She also knows how many calories she needs to stay within healthy guidelines. Every time I am with her, she enjoys a hamburger, confesses her love of Mexican food, and dabbles in a little chocolate. She does not deprive herself of those fun foods, but she eats them in moderation and is aware of what she is putting into her body. Discovering what your body needs and learning to become aware of what you eat is a life skill that will reap great benefits if you start early in life!

Another interesting fact I learned recently is that the food pyramid has changed quite a bit since I was in high school.

<table>
<tr><td>The pyramid used to look something like this:</td><td>Now it looks like this:</td></tr>
<tr><td>Illustration 4</td><td>Illustration 5</td></tr>
</table>

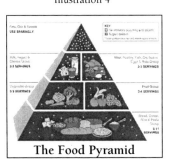

Source: http://tms.ecol.net/fitness/pyramid.html

Source: www.mypyramid.gov

The main difference is that the original pyramid introduced in 1992 sent a "one size fits all" message. Now there are twelve different versions, each slightly different, depending on a person's age, sex, and level of physical activity. You can actually find your personalized food pyramid at www.mypyramid. gov—it's fast and easy! The new pyramid also adds the activity element, which was absent from the original pyramid.

Finally, the biggest kicker out of my recent nutrition revelation was that water really is our best friend. First of all, it's calorie-free so we can drink as much of it as our little hearts desire. Secondly, our body really needs it—and lots of it. Drinking water is proven to help manage weight, improve skin, and provides us with energy throughout our days[33].

Eating in College

There are a myriad of factors that work against eating well in college. First of all, it's not like your dorm room has a gourmet kitchen. Keeping good snacks around for those *Grey's Anatomy* or *24* series marathons is tough if you don't have a refrigerator to store fresh fruit. Plus, every day is different—it's hard to keep a consistent schedule when you are in and out all the time. And let's be honest, the ongoing social gatherings and sorority meetings aren't going to provide you with great choices either. On top of this, you will most likely be on a tight budget. Healthy foods always seem to cost more in the grocery store than those grab-and-go kinds. Late night talks with friends, five-hour study sessions, and spontaneous celebrations allow you to put things in your mouth when you don't even realize you're eating because you are having so much fun! With a passion for this very subject, Daphine Oz, daughter of Oprah's Dr. Oz and college student at Princeton University, has put out a book with great information on healthier eating in college called *The Dorm Room Diet*. Throughout her book, she gives great tips on how to avoid those famous freshman fifteen, as well as beginning a healthy lifestyle while you're young (instead of having to undo bad habits after a major heart attack thirty years down the road). Some of the "grab and go" foods that she suggests having around are:

- instant oatmeal
- oat bran
- whole grain granola bars
- Chex, multi-bran or wheat cereals
- granola
- bagels
- crackers
- Melba toast
- fruit
- nuts
- veggies
- seltzer with a splash of fruit juice
- rice cakes

- soy crisps
- some chocolate[34]

I also enjoyed reading her five principles for healthy eating:

1. Always have breakfast.
2. Drink half your body weight in ounces of water daily—including one glass before every meal.
3. Eat at least every three hours(three meals/two snacks).
4. Count to your age before you "cheat."
5. Avoid eating within two hours of going to bed.[8]

Straight from a college student herself. She recognizes the fun in food, but by watching her dad's heart patients, she also knows what can happen if you are not aware of what you are putting in your mouth during college—you spend the rest of your life playing catch-up.

God gave us freedom to choose what we eat to fuel our bodies for His purposes. Be aware that the extremes exist. Be mindful of what you put in your mouth. And be joyful with every bite, knowing you are no longer under any law or set of rules that you must live by. At the end of the day, the goal is to keep our minds focused on Christ and not food.

Chapter Seven Reflection Questions

1. What is the biblical view of the way to see our bodies?

2. How does what we eat affect our daily lives?

3. What are differences in the way the Old Testament and the New Testament view food?

4. To which extreme are you more prone to be susceptible?

5. What are practical prevention measures or things you can do to prevent getting caught in a stronghold of either extreme?

6. If you struggle with a stronghold dealing with food, what is the real root of the problem that needs addressing before you leave for college?

Digging Deeper

■ What does the world tell us about our bodies?

- ■ What does the Bible tell us about our bodies?
  - Genesis 1:27
  - Isaiah 64:8
  - Psalm 139:13-14

- ■ What does the world say about beauty?

- ■ What does the Bible say about beauty?
  - Biblical characters described as beautiful:
    - Genesis 12:11 _____
    - Genesis 24:16 _____
    - 2 Samuel 11:2 _____
    - Esther 2:7 _____
  - Warning about beauty:
    - Proverbs 31:30 _____

- ■ Why is it important that we take good care of our bodies?
  - 1 Corinthians 6:15
  - 1 Corinthians 6:19-20

- ■ What does the Bible say about food?
  - Matthew 6:25-We don't need to _____ about what we eat.
  - Exodus 16:4-God will _____ all we need each day.

- Genesis 2:16-We should be able to eat
  _____.

- Proverbs 25:16-Our bodies will respond if
  we _____.

Chapter 8

. . . .

A BODY THAT MOVES

Exercise daily in God–no spiritual flabbiness,
please!

—1 Timothy 4:7MSG

This may sound strange, but our bodies were meant to move. If you think about it, not until recently did we have planes, trains, and automobiles to get us from point A to point B. Scripture suggests that back then they walked—a lot. Now that we are in the fast-paced world where we can do everything with a click of a mouse, we have to be a little more proactive when it comes to moving our bodies. In conjunction with the previous chapter about eating right, a healthy lifestyle (notice I didn't say health-nut lifestyle) involves getting some weekly or even daily exercise.

As I mentioned earlier, most high school athletes, cheerleaders, and dance teamers don't have the opportunity or even desire to continue such rigorous physical training in college. Up to this point, some kind of physical activity has been implanted in your day whether you knew it or not (even down to PE class). In the college world, you have to make time and effort for things such as exercise. The good news is that most college campuses have a state of the art fitness facility or are full of beautiful parks with walking and biking paths. Some might even still have "kinesiology" (what we would call PE) requirements.

Early on in college I enrolled in an aerobic walking class. I took it with a couple of girlfriends, and we had so much fun. Typically it was held in the morning, and we walked all around campus, up and down the football stadium, and got to catch up with each other in the meantime. I loved it so much I think I took it three times. What I needed was that scheduled block of time to "move." You may find other ways to keep active, such as:

- playing intramural sports
- jogging or biking through campus
- swimming in the natatorium
- attending classes such as spinning, kickboxing, or Pilates held through the fitness center

Just getting outside and throwing the frisbee around or choosing the stairs instead of the elevator are great ways to keep your body moving, your heart in shape, and your weight properly managed. Exercise has also been proven to be a great stress reliever. This is something that will come in handy as those mid-terms and finals roll around. My sister, a certified personal trainer and former fitness consultant, has a vast amount of knowledge when it comes to "moving the body." She recommends three things to consider when being purposeful about exercise:

- a **cardio workout** (so we can have a healthy heart),
- a **weight resistance workout** (so we can carry our own luggage), and
- a **stretching routine** (so we don't hurt ourselves in the meantime)

A weekly routine involving these three components will definitely improve your stature and put you on a path to a healthy lifestyle. On top of this regular "workout routine," she also recommends wearing a pedometer and walking 10,000 steps a day. Ten thousand steps = three miles, so challenge yourself to move around during the day and watch those steps add up!

Other benefits of exercising include lower stress levels, a more consistent digestive system, a healthier heart, less chance for disease, and stronger bones. However, just as we discussed in the eating section, a person can overdo it with exercise, too. Obviously, balance is the common thread here. Simply find an exercise that you enjoy, at a time when you are most energetic (it doesn't have to be at 6:00 A.M.), and you will begin building an active lifestyle to help you feel good, look good, and prevent disease.

Chapter Eight Reflection Questions

1. Why is it that some students find it harder to exercise in college than in high school?

2. What are some creative ways you might enjoy "moving" in college?

3. What are some practical reasons we need to continue exercising on a regular basis?

4. What are the three main components to remember when thinking up your exercise routine for the week?

5. Why is it important that we honor Christ with a balanced way of eating and exercising?

Chapter 9

THE BIG DEAL ABOUT ALCOHOL AND DRUGS

Everything is permissible for me—but not everything is beneficial—Everything is permissible for me—but I will not be mastered by anything.
—1 Corinthians 6:12

Alcohol—that word sure does get a lot of attention in high school, doesn't it? Well, it has a pretty big reputation in college, too. It's reported that four in five college students drink.[35] So, the big question—is alcohol bad? Is drinking wrong? And most importantly, what does the Bible say about it? At this point, you have already been faced with the decision of whether or not to take that drink. You have already earned a reputation–one way or another. The Department of Justice reported that in 2004 70.6 percent of high school seniors had consumed alcohol within that year.[36] No wonder the

Pennsylvania Liquor Control Board found in 2005 that "many students of higher education come to college with drinking patterns already in place."[37] But prepare yourself—the amount of alcohol you are around now is a drop in the bucket compared to what you will face when you are away from home in the college and university system.

By the time I was a senior in high school, my home state school of Louisiana State University was ranked the number one party school in America. I've always wondered how they came up with that statistic, but I sure did believe it. I was severely disappointed when I saw many friends older than I whom I truly respected get sucked into the unhealthy college party scene. At the time, alcohol was everywhere on that campus—not to mention that the drinking age was eighteen.

Alcohol is definitely a sensitive issue even in churches today, so let's get down to it. Is drinking wrong? Man, how I wish I could give you a black and white answer. Unfortunately, you have to make that decision for yourself. Let's go through a couple of scenarios (real-life stories with changed names to protect the innocent).

Scenario One:

Madison had what she thought was a normal childhood. Behind closed doors, though, her family had a big secret. Her dad was an alcoholic and no one else needed to know. Although her dad was a good father and involved in their lives, Madison swore she would never drink to prevent putting her own family in that situation. She kept that promise until she got to high school. One night, sleeping over with a friend, they wanted to experience something daring. Not a big deal to her at first, she had one drink, then another, then another, and sooner than later found herself really enjoying the "buzz" of not being able to think or feel any longer. She also discovered this new "life of the party" personality that her friends loved. The next weekend, she was right back in the scene, waiting for that "buzz" to kick in. Sure enough, this became the regular weekend routine habit. Not just to drink, but to get drunk. Soon, her body constantly craved the alcohol content, and without realizing it, she was officially addicted. One homecoming night, a devastating series of events involving bruises and school suspension made her realize she had a problem. She had officially become what she swore she never would—an alcoholic. After a week in a rehabilitation center with her family in Colorado, her addiction had finally been exposed. Upon returning home, a series of tough adjustments had to be made—her lifestyle, her friends, and her new way of having fun. Healing was a painful process, but it was the path she chose the rest of her senior year of high school and into her college years. What was one drink on one night became a regular weekend activity, then became a horrifying addiction. To this day, Madison has not had a sip of alcohol since her rehab experience.

Scenario Two:

Wherever there was Lindsay, there was fun. She lived on the edge and liked it there. She made good grades, had lots of friends, and life didn't intimidate her one bit. She was a believing Christian and faithfully went to church, but she got a little annoyed at the judgmental folks at school who automatically concluded that kids who drank were "rebellious heathens" and those who didn't were "good Christian kids." Being the youngest child in her family, there wasn't much she hadn't already seen. So when it came to drinking in high school, she didn't mind bending the rules a little. When older friends came home from college for the weekend, it was the usual routine for them to buy beer for the gang. Since she only drank one or two, her only fear was getting caught at parties by cops and being issued a minor in possession (MIP) ticket. Her friends did it—partly because it was rebellious, and partly because they liked feeling older than they really were. Lindsay never got drunk and never did anything wild with the guys; she just liked the taste of her drinks and the relaxed atmosphere, and she genuinely liked the people at the parties. Only problem was, she technically wasn't old enough. In time, her parents found out what was going on and expressed their deep disappointment, concern, and frustration with her. Still not really sure what the big deal was, she quit drinking for a time to appease her parents. A couple of years down the road, the college scene allowed her space from her parents to finally drink without them finding out. Again, she still wasn't old enough. Neither were the people she was with who were eventually caught by the police and issued MIPs that are now permanently on their records.

Scenario Three:

Jason was a good kid. Throughout his growing up years, he always noticed the "adult drinks" in his parents' cabinet. His parents were very good about talking to him about these adult drinks, and how they could harm a child or a student under a certain age. His parents didn't drink all the time, just at social events, dinner parties, and the occasional romantic dinner they cooked for each other. Beer was in the refrigerator, but his mom and dad only drank one at a time for rare occasions such as the Super Bowl and large family cookouts. An obedient child, Jason always followed the rules, respected his parents, and lived life within the boundaries provided for him. When Jason went off to college, he noticed that drinking was everywhere—at every football game, at every restaurant, at every fraternity party, and at almost everyone's apartment. He knew that the drinking age was twenty-one, but he was still eighteen. He didn't judge those around him who did drink; he just thought they were presumptuous to be drinking before the law said they could. He thoroughly enjoyed himself at all these events, and made lots of friends even though he wasn't actually sipping a beer. A few years passed, and Jason did finally turn twenty-one. His roommates made a big deal about the fact that he should go "party it up," but he knew better. He never had any intention of getting drunk, living off a temporary buzz, or using the excuse of drinking to keep up with any kind of popular crowd. Instead, he drank his first beer with a little disappointment in its horrible taste and decided he would stick to nice romantic dinners with a simple glass of wine.

Scenario Four:

Elizabeth never really saw gray. To her, issues like drinking were black and white. She saw two grandparents die of alcoholism and her dad had struggled with alcohol during his high school and college years. Since her dad's decision to become a Christian, alcohol was out of the picture and out of every cabinet in the house. With this background, Elizabeth viewed alcohol negatively and refused to be anywhere around it. Even as high school head cheerleader and class favorite, Elizabeth refused to attend after parties or get together after the games where alcohol was known to be present. Elizabeth was also very active in her church and boldly took a stand against drinking. As Elizabeth approached college, her standards did not change. She knew she was not of drinking age yet, she was aware of what alcohol had done to her family, and she just wasn't interested. Elizabeth sometimes struggled being in a sorority because drinking was somehow at all the events. She eventually got married, and on her honeymoon with her husband she enjoyed a few Hawaiian lava flows and after-dinner drinks. Elizabeth has chosen not to have alcohol in her home and usually avoids events where drinking is the main activity.

Okay, you get to decide. What are the positive and negative points in each scenario? Which scenario most describes you? Once you find your place, let's evaluate some truths about what we know about alcohol.

The Law

■ The legal age for alcohol in the USA is twenty-one years old. The National Minimum Drinking Age Act of 1984 required all states to raise their minimum purchase and public possession of alcohol age to twenty-one. States that did not comply faced a reduction in highway funds under the Federal Highway Aid Act. The U.S. Department of Transportation has determined that all states are in compliance with this act. The national law specifically prohibits purchase and public possession of alcoholic beverages [for those under the age of twenty-one].[38]

Staggering Statistics

■ The National Institute on Alcohol and Alcoholism reported staggering statistics of college students between the ages of eighteen and twenty-four.

- 1,700 college students die each year from alcohol-related unintentional injuries, including motor vehicle crashes.
- 599,000 students are unintentionally injured under the influence of alcohol.
- More than 696,000 students are assaulted by another student who has been drinking.
- More than 97,000 students are victims of alcohol-related sexual assault or date rape.
- 400,000 have unprotected sex and more than 100,000 report having been too intoxicated to know if they consented to having sex.
- About 25 percent of students report academic consequences of their drinking, including missing class, falling behind, doing poorly on exams or papers, and receiving lower grades overall.
- More than 150,000 reported developing alcohol-related health problems.
- 2.1 million students drive under the influence of alcohol each year.[39]

Random Facts

- A standard "drink" consists of:
  - One twelve-ounce bottle of beer or wine cooler,
  - One five-ounce glass of wine, or
  - 1.5 ounces of 80-proof distilled spirits[40]
- Binge drinking is defined as consuming five or more drinks in a row for men, and four or more drinks in a row for women.[41]

Illustration 6

- Two out of five college students are binge drinkers.[42]
- Binge drinking is associated with lower grades among college students. Approximately five drinks per occasion are associated with a grade point average (GPA) lowered by half a grade.[43]
- Each drink consumed by college students per occasion increased the probability of missing a class by 8 percent and getting behind in school by 5 percent.[44]

The amount of information available on under-age and college drinking is almost overwhelming. Hopefully, you are not oblivious to the fact that too much alcohol (too much of anything, really) can not only harm you, but those around you. Just as a quick review, the above information has told us that the drinking age in America is twenty-one. It also revealed that many car crashes, accidents, assaults, and date rapes occur when under the influence. And it shouldn't surprise you that drinking can actually affect your grades.

Maybe you are one of those people who looks at statistics and thinks, *That will never happen to me*. I pray it won't. But let's look at how these accidents, crashes, and sexual assaults actually take place. I can promise you that none of those victims ever intended their night of fun to end the way it did.

Whether you decide to go through rush and participate in sorority life or not, you will very likely be invited to fraternity or boys' club parties at some point in your college career. Of course, the scenario I am about to describe can be considered extreme and does not occur at all frat parties on every campus. However, this might give you a better idea of how what seems like an evening of innocent college fun can easily go wrong.

The College Drinking Scenario:

Coming home from an afternoon of studying at the library, you notice a bright orange piece of paper neatly rolled with a black ribbon hanging around your dorm room doorknob. Almost tossing it in the trash (thinking it would be another resident life noise level notice), you decide to go ahead and open it. At the top it reads:

YOU'VE BEEN CRUSHED.

BROTHERS OF THE XYZ FRATERNITY CORDIALLY INVITE YOU, _____, (*YOUR NAME CLEVERLY SCRIPTED BY A BOY'S HANDWRITING*) TO ATTEND OUR MOON FEVER HALLOWEEN CRUSH PARTY.

COSTUME OR NO COSTUME, PLEASE JOIN US AT ALL FAN'S PIZZA HOUSE STARTING AT 8:00 P.M. NEXT FRIDAY FOR A NIGHT OF TERRIFYING FEATS AND LOTS OF DANCING.

Flattered and very excited, you immediately text message your friend to see if she got the same invitation. Soon after, the costumes are bought and finally a night of Halloween terror and fun is around the corner. Upon entering what you thought was a pizza place, you discover a well-decorated spook zone complete with strobe lights, dry ice smoke, and hopping dance floor. Guys are everywhere, and the dance floor is just begging you and your friend (who are appropriately dressed up as eighties aerobics dancers complete with high side ponytails) to boogie down to Michael Jackson's classic *Thriller*. After working up a small sweat with the crowd on the dance floor, a nice looking guy wearing only a tuxedo bow tie, cummerbund, and black pants passes out little containers of Jell-O while dancing into the next song. Cool, you think to yourself. Jell-O shots…that's just the little sugar boost I need for the next dance. They are so tasty, you have three or four. Having worked up a full-blown sweat, you and the crowd around you decide to hop on over to get a drink to cool you off a little. A diet coke sounds best, but no sodas are to be found. The bartender screams over the music and strobe lights, "What'll it be?" Hm, you've never really done this before since you are still just eighteen, so you uncomfortably ask to have what "they" are having. Before you know it, a beer is in hand and the crowd you are with is making its way back to the dance floor.

A couple more groups join the girls giddily dancing to "Girls Just Want to Have Fun" when some creepy guy asks if you want to have some REAL fun tonight. Completely weirded out, you turn away and grab the friend you came with, laughing about what just happened. Dying of thirst at this point, you go and get another beer. Hiding in a corner to get a break from some of the weirdo guys who have attempted to grind you in your dancing circle, a fresh face with a friendly smile takes your beer and says, "You want to get some fresh air?" He leads you to the back patio, where smokers are leaning against rails and folks are telling stories between belly laughs. Trying to feel comfortable without your sidekick around, you and this nice guy actually hold a decent conversation for a good ten minutes. Eventually, he hands you back your beer, and you nervously sip until Usher's "Yeah!" starts blaring, and back to the dancing circle he takes you. The next thing you know, you wake up in the fraternity house without your clothes in some guy's bed—but he's not there. What in the world just happened?

You've just become a statistic.

So, let's replay this truly terrifying scenario, and in all seriousness discuss what was really going on. First of all, the Jell-O shots were made with vodka (not water), so the four "sugar boosts" you just swallowed were more like alcohol appetizers. Then, without much food in your stomach, you drank a beer (completely aware that you and most everyone else in that place was underage). After a while, you drank another beer. The only catch is, when that "guy" took it away from you, he dropped Rohypnol in your bottle and waited for it to dissolve before giving it back to you. Your memory is blank from that point, but his fun was not. He took you back to his room at the frat house and had sex with you. The only reason you can figure this out is through the soreness and bleeding in that area since you had been a virgin. You have been sexually assaulted and violated beyond your worst nightmare.

Talk about scary.

Thank goodness it didn't really just happen.

That is why alcohol in the college scene gets so much attention. It's not just about a beer. It's about tricky Jell-O shots, date rape drugs, and guys who are out there waiting for you to get drunk so they can have their way with you. It's about car crashes, violent outbursts during love quarrels, and even rape. So if you were to go back and rewrite that story, how would it read? What are things you could have done to prevent the unthinkable from happening?

Drinking is just the beginning of questionable issues in college. Other college scenarios that may present you with a tough decision include using fake ID's to get into clubs and hooka parties (getting buzzed on "natural" tobacco). Just don't even go there. Hooka parties could easily lead to a serious drug problem down the road. When people get bored with the alcohol buzz or the hooka buzz they will most likely turn to more powerful substances. Marijuana and cocaine seem to be the most popular college drug choices.[45] Growing in media attention are substances such as painkillers and prescribed drugs. Regardless of how tough college becomes or how frustrating life can be in general, these are more of Satan's traps to lure you into worldly pleasures and escapes that are not only temporary, but also violently addicting. When things as serious as drugs enter the college picture, my best advice to you is to flee. In 2 Timothy 2:22, it states, "Flee the evil desires of the youth, and pursue righteousness, faith, love, and peace, along with those who call on the Lord out of a pure heart." Any time you are in an uncomfortable place with questionable people around dangerous things, by all means LEAVE.

Now that you know the facts, the statistics, the danger of the alcohol scene, and the other things it can lead to, let's look more at what the Bible says about alcohol. According to Daniel Witfield, author of an article "Alcohol and the Bible," an estimated 228 references to wine occur in the Bible and nineteen more reference "strong drink"…for a total of 247 total verses on the subject.[46] In his research, he tagged these verses into three broad categories: positive references, negative references, and neutral references. Here's what he found:

- Total negative references: forty (16 percent)
  - seventeen warnings against abusing alcohol
  - nineteen examples of people abusing alcohol
  - three references to selecting leaders
  - one reference to abstaining if it causes a brother to stumble

- Total positive references: 149 (59 percent)
  - fifty-nine references to the practice of drinking alcohol with a meal.
  - twenty-seven references to the abundance of wine as an example of God's blessing
  - twenty-five references to the use of wine in offerings and sacrifices
  - nine references as wine being a gift
  - five metaphorical references to wine as a basis for favorable comparison.

COLLEGE BOUND ON SOLID GROUND

■ Total neutral references: sixty-two (25 percent)
  • thirty-three symbolic references
  • twenty-one references to vows of abstinence
  • four references of people falsely accused of being drunk
  • four references which don't seem to fit a category.

Interesting? I thought so. Of course, other factors can be debated about drinking in Jesus' day such as: was it really wine (or just grape juice), was the water so polluted that wine was the drink of choice out of necessity, and what is the true definition of "drunkenness"? I'll let you draw your own conclusions and dig deeper into this issue as you see necessary for finding your own convictions. In the meantime, here are some commonly known stories and verses you will most likely encounter in college.

Commonly Known Bible Verses on Alcohol

  • "Do not join those who drink too much wine or gorge themselves on meat, for drunkards and gluttons become poor, and drowsiness clothes them in rags." Proverbs 23:20, 21
  • Jesus turned water into wine during the first miracle of His public ministry. John 2:1-11
  • Jesus broke bread and drank wine during the last supper with His disciples. Luke 22:7-38

- "Let us behave decently, as in the daytime, not in orgies and drunkenness, not in sexual immorality and debauchery, not in dissension and jealousy." Romans 13:13
- "Do not get drunk on wine, which leads to debauchery. Instead, be filled with the spirit." Ephesians 5:18

Overall, does the Bible say drinking is wrong? No. Does the Bible say getting drunk is wrong? Yes. There you have it. When it comes to drinking, many adults argue about where that fine line lies. The Bible obviously leaves that up to you. The definite instructions we have are to obey the law (Romans 13:1) and to not get drunk (Ephesians 5:18). You have to set your own parameters from there. I do know that if you are constantly seeking God's will and pursuing a life filled with the fruit of the Spirit, then He will guide and lead you to draw boundaries appropriate for yourself. If you struggle with that decision now, it will only be magnified in college when you are out of your parents' protection. Alcohol will be everywhere in college—everywhere. Decide now your boundaries if you haven't already. Your college experience is meant to be wonderful and exciting, but waking up to a horrific tragedy or spending a semester in rehab is not my idea of wonderful and exciting. Pray about it—the Spirit will lead you to what is best.

Chapter Nine Reflection Questions

1. What was your family's view of alcohol while you were growing up?

2. What is the Bible's view of alcohol?

3. Why is it important to have your boundaries set before going to college?

4. What are benefits to drinking?

5. What are drawbacks to drinking?

6. Of the four scenarios presented, which one best describes you and why? What will it be in college?

7. What shocked you most about the college fraternity scenario?

8. After praying about this and seeking out God's Word, what will be your stance on drinking in college and in life?

Digging Deeper

More about what the Bible says when it comes to drinking: (using the New International Version will help fill in the blanks more easily)

■ Verses that have *positive things* to say about it:

- Psalm 104:14, 15
  He makes wine that _____ the heart of man.

- Isaiah 55:1
  Come all you who are thirsty...and buy _____.

- John 2:1-11
  Jesus turns water into _____ in His first miracle.

- Luke 22:7-28
  Christ offered _____ to the disciples at the last supper to represent His blood that would be shed for them.

■ Verses that warn *against* drinking:

- Proverbs 20:1
  Whoever is led astray by beer and wine is not _____.

- Proverbs 23:20
  Do not join those who _____.

- Ephesians 5:18
  Do not get _____ on wine.

- Proverbs 23:29-35
  Who has woe, sorrow, strife, and complaints…
  those who linger over _____.

- Galatians 5:19
  The acts of the sinful nature are _____:
  sexual immorality, impurity and debauchery,
  idolatry and witchcraft, hatred, jealousy,
  discord, fits of rage, selfish ambition, dissen-
  tion, factions, and envy, _____,
  orgies…and the like.

■ Other verses that should be considered:

- Romans 13:1
  We are to _____ to our authorities.

- Ephesians 6:1-3
  Children, _____ your parents.

- John 14:23
  If anyone loves me, he or she will _____
  my teaching.

- Romans 14:17-18
  The kingdom is not a matter of eating or
  drinking, but of_____,
  _____, and _____
  in the Holy Spirit.

. . . .

SEX AND
THE COLLEGE CITY

For by Him all things were created: things
in heaven and on earth, visible and invisible,
whether thrones or powers or rulers or authorities; all things were created by him and for him.
He is before all things, and in Him all things
hold together.

—Colossians 1:16-17

When you were a small child, did your parents
have strict rules about not playing near or
in the street? Mine did. And I didn't take it
that seriously until one day my 6'7" dad found me
fetching a basketball that had rolled right into the
middle of one with a car coming. Thank goodness
my dad was watching and came to my rescue. The
spanking and the lecture left quite an impression
on me, and I don't think I ever did it again. Was his

rule of not playing in the street to keep me from having fun? Was it to make me resentful of him? Was it to set me up for failure? Of course not! My dad loved me and wanted to keep me safe. He wanted to protect me from getting run over by any cars that drove too fast down our street. Later on when I was in late elementary school, he looked at me and said, "I don't care if you and your friends play kickball in the street, just watch for cars and be careful." At that point, he knew I was old enough to watch out for cars and stay safe. So what does this have to do with sex?

God designed sex to be wonderful, beautiful, and fun—but not until we are ready. God is simply protecting us by asking us to wait for marriage until we have sex. According to His Word, we are not ready until we have completely committed our lives to one person in a marriage relationship. In the same way my dad wanted to protect me from getting hurt or killed with his rules about playing in the street, so is God with giving us sexual boundaries in the Bible. He knows how great sex is—He invented it. But we might get hurt or killed if we are playing somewhere we shouldn't be before we are ready.

Why Is It So Tempting?

Have you ever counted the number of television commercials that are attempting to sell something simple like a piece of gum, a hair highlighting kit, or a power tool when across the screen walks a six-foot long and lean body barely dressed in a bikini with flowing locks and a lip gloss overdose to deliver the final lines in the ad? What's going on? I thought this was about a power drill? How many e-mails do you delete each week, knowing that if you opened this random address, a pornographic video would pop up? Or how many scantily clad women do you see stretched across the billboards on the side of the road (which, by the way, you never quite catch what they are selling because the words are too small)? Let's face it—our culture is obsessed with sex. Why are these ad campaigns successful and "adult video" parking lots always full? Because sex is a tempting, available, and powerful tool to use on people in a culture obsessed with beauty, fame, and pleasure. It's attractive not only because it's everywhere, but it's the ultimate teenage "no-no." Much like alcohol can be, what we are told we cannot have is the very thing we want the most. The mystery of it is what marketers bank on you falling for.

God created sex, and it is meant to be extremely pleasurable and awesome—and everything else you can imagine it would be! Genesis 2:24 tells us we are to wait until we are united in marriage to become one flesh. God has a beautiful and divine purpose in allowing both men and women great pleasure in becoming one flesh in the act of sex. Because the enemy has invaded our culture, the sin of man has perverted this most beautiful marital act into a social event that supposedly elevates your social status and deepens your relationship with the opposite sex. As attractive as all that sounds, it's a lie. And ladies, the Bible is very clear about sexual boundaries for your protection—not for your embarrassment or torture.

Why Is It So Controlling?

There are three different crowds I invite to the table for this discussion: those who have already engaged in sexual activity, those who have gone as far as you can go without "going all the way," and those who have not yet gone either of those places physically but think about it all the time. Notice that I am not inviting anyone to the table who has never had an impure thought or sexual act. If I tried to do that, no one would show up for this discussion. All of us are drawn to this mystery of sex in one way or another.

I recently completed a Bible study led by Beth Moore on the book of Daniel. In this study, our class took a close look at the Babylonian culture, which is very similar to the culture we live in today. It was the dominating world power at the time; the people lived in extreme luxury; and they were obsessed with beauty, youth, and material things. In one video session, this powerful study teaches that there are many areas Satan loves to attack us in, but sexual sin is his favorite. Beth Moore goes on to explain that sexual sin is Satan's specialty in keeping humans in bondage to sin because of the shame, embarrassment, and pain that it can bring to us. Satan uses this special type of sin to make us feel unworthy of God's grace, unable to be forgiven, and not useful for the kingdom. She then reveals how God in His great goodness can break these strongholds, and in Him we can be made new again.

Before I go any further, let me right now speak to those of you at this table who have engaged in sexual activity and who are not married yet. You are VERY worthy of His grace, you are ALREADY forgiven (all you have to do is ask), and you will FOREVER be useful for the kingdom if you are seeking God's will for your life. If you have succumbed to Satan's lies about sex, there is hope, forgiveness, and new beginnings waiting for you. Our God is a great God who is in love with the worst of sinners—and that is all of us! Don't let the pain and shame of hidden sexual sin or overt sexual relationships keep you in bondage any longer. If you are currently in a relationship with a guy who is using this tool to control you, manipulate you, or simply use you—you are still a child of God who is not bound by the stronghold of Satan's lies, but by a God who sent His very Son to die for you. Ask God this day to release you from this stronghold and begin pursuing a life that is full of wonderful, lovely things that bring truth and freedom to your life.

Those of you at this table who are experimenting and playing with sexual fire—be warned. Don't think you are so clever you can outwit our enemy with justification, keeping things quiet, or going as far as you can without "really having sex." Even those of you who may have never even had a boyfriend, but enjoy self pleasure in the secret of your own bed—this can still have power over you. Simply put, it is really hard to have an intimate relationship with God when you have this kind of activity separating you from Him. You can also be free from any stronghold, and new beginnings are waiting for you, too. All you have to do is ask. God longs to meet with you every day, show you wonderful things, and give you a life of abundance. But He can't when He is not your stronghold and these other things are. Surrender yourself to Him and enjoy the freedom in knowing that sex is absolutely fabulous when your partner is a man who loves you unconditionally, is going to be with you for the rest of your life, and isn't interested in "tell all" sessions with the boys in the locker room or frat house.

Why Is It So beautiful?

Sex is so beautiful because God created it. He designed for a husband and a wife to be enraptured with each other in unending sexual pleasure within the bounds of marriage. The marriage bed has no boundaries except for what is comfortable for you and your mate—how cool is that! What a creative way for us to fill the earth and multiply. In time, you will most likely be able to fully embrace the God-given desires and feelings that are inside of you. Only by the grace of God am I able to share with you how truly beautiful it is when you make that special honeymoon night worth the wait!

Consequences of Sex Before Marriage

What exactly can happen if you do have sex before marriage? I love the way the authors of *Lady in Waiting* clearly define four specific areas of your life that are affected when fornication (or sex before marriage) occurs. They explain how having sex before marriage affects you physically, emotionally, relationally, and spiritually.[47] Let's explore these.

Physical Damage

You are probably most familiar with the effects premarital sex can have in the physical sense.

• STDs

A sexually transmitted disease (STD) is the most common physical problem that occurs. In fact, there are more than twenty-five of them that have created a significant public health challenge in the United States.[48] In short, there are two main types—bacterial and viral. The most common bacterial STDs, such as chlamydia, gonorrhea, syphilis, and trichomonaisis, can be treated and cured with antibiotics if caught early enough. Viral STDs, such as herpes (HSV -2), hepatitis B, HIV, and the human papillomavirus (genital warts) are not curable. They have life-long symptoms and can even lead to death in their worst stages. Here are some interesting statistics about STDs:

- 63 percent of all sexually transmitted disease cases occur among people under twenty-five years of age.[49]
- The Center for Disease Control estimates that 19 million new infections occur each year, almost half of them among young people, ages fifteen to twenty-four.[50]

• Pregnancy

Naturally, any time sex occurs there is a possibility of becoming pregnant. And we all know that until we have a husband, we are not ready for that responsibility! In *The King's Daughter*, Dianna Hagee states that,

> [Sex] has a purpose and a supernatural definition of what it is {a bonding between husband and wife during which the two become one}, what it is for {procreation and pleasure for a husband and a wife}, and what God intended it to be {which is clearly expressed in the Song of Solomon}.[51]

Okay, that word *procreation* means to populate the earth. Or get pregnant. In other words, one reason God created sex was to allow a woman to get pregnant and have a baby. If you are not ready for this possibility, you are not ready for sex. This is a huge reason why we are given the instruction to wait until marriage to have sex. Unfortunately, Satan has, of course, come to pervert the truth with his lies, so he justifies premarital sex with "safe sex" campaigns through the use of condoms, the "pill," and other forms of birth control. Here are some more interesting facts:

- The pill fails 6.2 percent of the time
- The condom fails 14.2 percent of the time.
- The diaphragm fails 15.6 percent of the time
- Spermicide fails 26.3 percent of the time.
- Early college-age women show the highest percentage of contraceptive failure during the first 12 months of use (25.9 percent). Later college-age women ranked second, not far behind (18 percent).[52]
- In 2000, 13 percent of all pregnancies, or 831,000, occurred among adolescents aged fifteen to nineteen.[53]

God did not intend for us to live our lives with a myriad of STD's and a baby before we were ready. Wait for the right mate, and you won't have to worry about any of these things. Isn't that good news?

Emotional Damage

An old saying goes, "Guys give love to get sex; girls give sex to get love." As girls, we are the more emotional human beings. We long to be loved, adored, respected, and treated like a princess. These things are usually much higher on our priority list than physical needs, even in a marriage relationship.

Unfortunately, sometimes girls will have sex with a guy in order to get that feeling of being loved. This is another one of Satan's tricky lies. Once you do cross that barrier and give yourself fully to someone else, you are bonded. They then have a part of you. When an unmarried relationship becomes too physical, in come doubt and fear.

- Will he still love me?
- Did it satisfy him?
- Will we still get married?
- Does he love me just because we had sex?
- Will anyone find out?
- Am I pregnant?[54]

Questions such as these start to consume you. This is not the kind of relationship God had in mind for you. A true, loving, godly relationship is based on trust, respect, and encouragement. Those things are polluted when pre-marital sex enters the picture. The emotional strings that attach themselves between two people after a sexual experience are only intended to stay attached for life. Imagine gluing two pieces of paper together and letting the glue dry. After a few hours, it would be impossible to pull apart those two pieces of paper again without some tearing and ripping involved. In the same way, sex can be considered the "glue" that bonds a marriage together. When this type of bond occurs between to two people who eventually break up, the toll in the tearing and ripping of the heart leaves painful scars.

Relational Damage

When guys ask you out on a date or want to pursue you, there is a profound "mystery" to you that they want to discover. Smart girls don't let them discover everything until the honeymoon, or even afterwards. Once a shallow guy knows everything there is to know about you, his interest is lost, the mystery is gone, and the relationship usually goes kaput.

In a dating relationship, one of the most fun components is building a genuine friendship. Getting to know each other's hobbies, favorite restaurants, favorite movies, and personality quirks make dating interesting and exciting. When sex enters the picture, somehow the friendship begins to dwindle and what brought you together in the first place is lost. Consider a guy's perspective of how this happened to him in an article titled, "College, Sex, & Love":

> I had a college sweetheart, the girl of my dreams. With her, there was never a dull moment. We totally "clicked." We waited for a while, then, through my initiation we started having sex. Sex soon became the focus of our relationship. I stopped wanting to get to know her on any other level. And so, instead of growing closer together, we actually started drifting apart. That's what

I mean by "sex killed my best relationships." People can relate on different levels—emotionally, mentally, physically, and spiritually. But when my girlfriend and I started relating mostly physically, it short-circuited the other parts of our relationship. As a result, the relationship as a whole started to go south. We might still be together today if we (I) had waited.[55]

Not only does sex before marriage affect your current relationship, it can affect your future relationships as well. If you are in a sexual relationship right now, think of your partner as someone's future husband. Someone's future father. One day, you will likely get married and what will you tell your husband on your honeymoon? What will you tell your children when they ask you if you waited until you got married? They are all fair questions. What will be your answer?

Spiritual Damage

The hardest hit when sexual sin enters a person's life is the distance it brings between you and God. God clearly states in His Word His boundaries for us in the sexual arena:

- "For you know what instructions we gave you by the authority of the Lord Jesus. It is God's will that you should be sanctified: that you should avoid sexual immorality; that each of you should learn to control his own body in a way that is holy and honorable, not in passionate lust like the heathen, who do not know God." 2 Thessalonians 4:2-7

- "Marriage should be honored by all, and the marriage bed kept pure, for God will judge the adulterer and all the sexually immoral." Hebrews 13:4
- "Flee from sexual immorality…" 1 Corinthians 6:18
- "But among you, there must not be even a hint of sexual immorality, or of any kind of impurity, or of greed, because these are improper for God's holy people." Ephesians 5:3
- "Put to death, therefore, whatever belongs to your earthly nature: sexual immorality, impurity, lust, evil desires, and greed, which is idolatry. Because of these, the wrath of God is coming." Colossians 3:5-6

Committing sexual sin such as lust, fornication (having sex before marriage), and adultery (having sex with someone other than your husband when you are married) hurt your relationship with God. Also, when you are in a sexual relationship, it hurts your reputation and your ability to witness to people about Christ. Thankfully, God is always extending His hand to bring you back into His presence. If you know that you need to come back to Him, please do. Confess to Him now that you recognize the sin in which you have become entangled, and receive the gift of mercy and grace that He has waiting for you. It's never too late to make it right with God.

Sex in College

In 2005, 47 percent of high school students admitted to having intercourse.[56] An article from the Christian Broadcast Network Web site recently revealed that "Most college young people are involved in sexual activity of some type or the other. At least 75 percent have been involved in sexual intercourse."[57] Wow. Did you miss that huge percentage jump? Not only am I shocked at the number of high schoolers having sex, look at how many more become sexually active in college. Why so many?

Quite frankly the accountability that you have during your high school years under your parents' roof is removed during your college years. *You* get to decide when you come in for the night. There won't be mom or dad "checking in" on you when you're at a guy's apartment after a date or party. It's just *you and him*.

Girls often like to talk about boundaries and "How far is too far?" I think that is a great discussion to have. Only you can make that decision for you. What you feel like is honoring to the Lord (or dishonoring) may be different from someone else. But I encourage you to set your boundaries now. Know your limits and don't let any guy talk you into going any further. Think about the things in a relationship that could easily lead to sex and try to avoid those situations. For example:

- You are at your boyfriend's dorm room and his roommate is out of town. You watch a movie until late into the night. Should you go ahead and spend the night or have him walk you back to your dorm?
- You and the guy you are dating decide to study together since you are in the same chemistry class. After a few hours, he decides to take a nap and wants you to snuggle with him. Are you going to lie down and nap next to him on the couch or grab a bite to eat while he's sleeping?

These are a few of many examples of why college is such an easy place to let down your guard and loosen up your buttons—I mean boundaries.

In *Every Woman's Battle*, Shannon Ethridge shares more about boundaries and vulnerable areas to look out for when it comes to sexual temptation. She boils these vulnerable areas down to three things:

- Compromising clothing
- Compromising company
- Compromising actions[58]

Guarding yourself against sexual temptation in college and setting healthy boundaries begins long before that "should I or shouldn't I moment." Take a close look at what you are wearing, whom you are hanging out with, and what you are saying and doing. Do these things indicate a child of God? Are these things representative of something holy and pleasing to the Lord? Instead of putting on a tank top that shows a little cleavage, a skirt that you know is way too short, or a pair of jeans that is so low your crack is your cleavage…put on the full armor of God as represented in Ephesians chapter six.

Making new friends in college is one of the best parts—make sure that you are attracting the right kind. And take a minute to think through the potential consequences of the many spontaneous ideas you come up with that sound exciting—will you regret it when you wake up in the morning…or in years to come? Setting your boundaries now (if you haven't already) will be the difference between you and other college girls who fumble and fall into Satan's sexual lies and strongholds.

And finally…

One last word about sex and the college scene. A common reason college students are likely to get heavily involved in sexual activity is directly related to alcohol. One report revealed that, "Many college kids throw themselves into soulless sex, a series of meaningless sexual encounters, often fueled by almost killer amounts of alcohol." Later the same report went on to say, "Drinking is probably the paramount reason that there seems to be a different sexual ethos on campus, as opposed to everywhere else on the planet."[59]

It should come as no surprise that alcohol and sex frequently go hand in hand (as seen in the last chapter) in the college scene. Setting both alcohol and sexual boundaries is a critical part of your college success.

It's funny how a little three-letter word can have so much power. What God meant for His glory and multiplying to fill the earth, Satan has used to ruin lives and relationships. Protect yourself, your relationships, and your future by taking time to answer the following questions before you go to college. I promise you will be glad you did.

Chapter Ten Reflection Questions

1. What are ways you didn't even realize you were being protected from sexual temptation by living under your parents' roof?

2. Are you currently in bondage to any secret or overtly sexual sin? If so, please talk to someone you trust and ask God for forgiveness and freedom in this area before you go to college. The stronghold only magnifies as time goes on.

3. Do you wear compromising clothing?

4. Do you tend to hang out with compromising company?

5. Do you say and do compromising things?

6. What are going to be your new sexual boundaries when you go off to college?

Digging Deeper

- *Who* invented sex?
  - _____ did! Colossians 1:16-17 Why?
    - To be fruitful and _____ . Genesis 1:28
    - For husband and wife to become_____. Genesis 2:24
    - His commandments concerning sexual boundaries exist so that we might_____ and be _____. Deuteronomy 6:20-25

- *Why* does our culture focus on it so much?
  - What God meant for His glory, Satan is out to _____, _____, and _____. John 10:10

- Human nature without the Holy Sprit does what the flesh desires, not what _____ desires. Romans 8:5
- Unfortunately, sex sells. But you, as a believer, know better than to buy into it.

■ *Where* is the real damage done?
  - Spiritually
    - There is a separation between you and God. Why? He gives us specific instructions and warnings when it comes to our sexual boundaries:
      - "We should _____ sexual immorality." 1 Thessalonians 4:2-7
      - "The marriage bed should be kept _____." Hebrews 13:4
      - "_____ from sexual immorality...." 1 Corinthians 6:18
      - "There must not be even a _____ of sexual immorality." Ephesians 5:3
      - "Put to death whatever belongs to your _____ nature: sexual immorality, _____, _____...." Colossians 3:5-6
    - Your reputation is tainted, which hurts your witness for Christ.

■ *When* can I make it right with God if I have already made this mistake?

- It's never too late!
  - God is the God of new beginnings…all you have to do is ask. 1 John 1:9
  - Moving on may require dealing with the consequences, but in Christ you don't have to deal with guilt or condemnation. Keep on the right track! Hebrews 12:1

PART THREE
GROWING IN THE SPIRITUAL LIFE

And Jesus grew in wisdom and stature, and *in favor with God* and men.

—Luke 2:52

In generations before us, college was seen as an excuse to check out of the spiritual world and live it up to the fullest for a few years without much consequence. Sowing the wild oats, if you will. In recent years, however, an overwhelming wave of revival has washed over many college campuses, bringing a refreshing spiritual rain in the hearts of college students around the world.

With estimations that somewhere between 65 and 94 percent of high school students stop attending church upon entering college, many high school seniors wonder if it is possible to stay connected to Christ during college.[60] You bet it is. Nothing delights our Lord more. What better time than now to chew on all the questions you have probably been afraid to ask about God? What better time than now to figure out what you believe and why? What better time than now to equip yourself with the tools to share the gospel with those God places in your path? And what better time to discover your spiritual gifts that allow you to serve the Father in ways you never dreamed possible?

Maybe you have been a Christian since you were a small child and are already walking in the ways of Truth, fully expecting college to be a challenging faith ride. Great—don't skip the next few chapters. Maybe you just want to survive college and you picked this up to grab a few hints. Great—don't skip the next few chapters. Maybe you have been turned off by Christianity lately because of the hypocrites in your high school that show up to church on Sundays and Wednesday nights but party all weekend. Great—don't skip the next few chapters. For those in the last category, Rob Bell, creator of the *Nooma* video series, poses perhaps the most pivotal question to our generation, "Is it possible to be interested in Christian faith but turned off by Christianity?"[61] Absolutely. Christianity is not about a set of rules of do's and don'ts. Christianity is about following Christ, loving people, and living life by connecting on a personal level with our Creator. Unfortunately, we as Christians can get caught up in the pomp and circumstance of church, religion, and rules.

Wherever you are in your faith, I urge you to keep an open mind as you read the next few chapters. I love the way A.W. Tozer puts it in his famous little book call *The Pursuit of God*:

> I want deliberately to encourage this mighty longing after God. The lack of it has brought us to our present low estate. The still and wooden quality about our religious lives is a result of our lack of holy desire. Complacency is a deadly foe of all spiritual growth. Acute desire must be present or there will be no manifestation of Christ to His people. He wants to be wanted. Too bad that with many of us He waits so long, so very long, in vain.[62]

All the other areas we are discussing are indeed important, but nothing holds a candle to the importance of having a personal relationship with Jesus Christ. No other area will seem fulfilling if this one major piece is missing. Colossians 1:17 tells us, "He is before all things, and in Him all things hold together." He is in all these areas, bringing true purpose and balance to it all. Yes, pursuing God and getting connected to a spiritual community are definitely worthy of a whole leg on our four-legged table; but in reality, He is in all things.

In my experience, students usually polarize to one extreme or another on these issues in college. Some folks turn away from God, thinking He will prevent them from having true college fun while questioning everything about religion and if there even is a God. Others tend to polarize in the other direction and the building of their faith really takes off in a positive direction. They are intrigued and curious to know more about their own faith and grow with the Lord during their college years.

Into which area do you want to fall? Are you going to turn your back on God, or do you want to draw nearer to Him? College professors, college students, and the college atmosphere purposely lead you to think about things you have never had to think about before. Allow the questions you have make you seek His face for answers. Allow your spirit and mind to be challenged as you dig into His Word. And allow this special time to let go of depending on your family's faith and start believing and living it on your own. This is not always popular or easy, but it has great rewards when you least expect it.

Chapter 11

* *

WHOSE FAITH IS IT
ANYWAY?

But in your hearts set apart Christ as Lord.
Always be prepared to give an answer to everyone
who asks you to give the reason for the hope
that you have.

—1 Peter 3:15

I'll never forget the night I was transferred from
my over-assignment temporary dorm room to
the one I would be living in for the rest of my
freshman year. After a long month of living on a
stow-away bed with a hanging rack as a closet (being
the "over-assigned" third wheel in a two-person
dorm room), I was thrilled to have my own bed and
my own drawer space. Little did I know that I was
about to go on a faith journey like none other when
I knocked on my new door.

125

My new roommate, Pratima, cheerfully invited me in as if she had been waiting on me all that time. We exchanged smiles, and I couldn't get over all the blank space in the room that would soon be mine. After moving a few boxes and making my bed, I sat down with a sigh to organize my nightstand area. On top I put a lamp, a few pictures of my family, and my teal Bible that I had been given in the seventh grade. I could tell Pratima was fixated on this, so I asked her if she was a Christian. She bluntly cut me off and explained that she was from India—and a devout Hindu. This should have been very clear to me, but I had not yet received the bathroom tour with the various written meditations, prayers, and spiritual figurines neatly placed along the mirror and counter. To soften the conversation, I asked her a few questions about her background, but then she cut me off again. After walking over and picking my Bible up, she looked at me square in the eye and asked me, "Why do you believe what you believe?"

A deafening silence hit the room as I had never been asked that exact question. I knew I had asked Jesus to come into my heart at age fifteen (and I could tell her about that). I knew that I had gone to church my whole life (and I could tell her about that). And I knew that our country was founded on biblical principles (with her being from India, I could easily go into that)…but that was not what she was asking.

To break the silence, she asked again, "Why do you believe in your God?" This time she changed it up a bit. *Your God*, I thought? How could there be more than one God? For the next three hours, we sat down and quizzed each other back and forth on our faiths. I soon learned that she knew all about Jesus —as much or more than I did. Embarrassed, I knew nothing about the Hindu faith—which haunted and bothered me. That night changed the way I viewed and lived out my faith. I spent the next four years in college making my faith my own. Figuring out why I believed what I believed. No one had ever challenged me like that—let alone the person I would be living with for the next eight months. Although I had become a Christian a few years earlier, it was time that I let go of the idea that the Christian faith was right because I grew up that way, because my parents believed, or because that's just the way Americans believe. Not anymore. *I* wanted to learn about all the other religions, what they believed, and have a renewed confidence that my Lord and Savior was THE ONLY Lord and Savior. I even wanted to visit other denominations and study the difference in doctrines of churches that all believe that Christ is Lord.

The truly exciting part is that this journey never ends. I am still learning, experiencing, studying, and discovering all the mysteries of our God. And just so you know, I still don't have all the answers…no one will until we are face to face with Him in heaven!

I encourage you to take a deep look into your heart and soul as you prepare to leave for college. What do you believe? Why do you believe it? Why do you attend the church you attend? Are you familiar with other religions and why they think their god is the only god?

Rose Publishing puts out an incredible pamphlet called *Christianity, Cult, and Religions* that describes in detail key information about cults and other religions. Using this great information, below is a summary of some key cults and religions you will very likely encounter during your college years.

The Cults (Off-shoots of Christianity)

Mormonism (Latter-day Saints)

The Church of Jesus Christ of Latter-day Saints was formed by Joseph Smith in 1830 in New York. Currently the headquarters are located in Salt Lake City, Utah. This sect uses *The Book of Mormon, Doctrine and Covenants, Pearl of Great Price* along with the Bible (The King James version or Smith's "inspired" version), and other authoritative teachings of Mormon prophets. Under this teaching, there is no trinity (God, Jesus, and the Holy Spirit are three separate gods) and worthy men may one day become gods themselves. The death of Jesus on the cross did not provide full atonement for all sin, but does provide everyone with a resurrection. They teach that we are resurrected by grace, but saved (exalted to godhood) through good works. There is no eternal life without Mormon membership. Eventually nearly everyone goes to one of three separate heavenly "kingdoms," with some achieving godhood. Alcohol, tobacco, coffee, and tea are forbidden, and baptism is on behalf of the dead. A two-year missionary commitment is encouraged.

Jehovah's Witnesses

Jehovah's Witnesses (known as the Watchtower Bible and Tract Society) was founded by Charles Taze Russell (who later became Joseph F. Rutherford) in 1879 in Pennsylvania. The headquarters currently remain in Brooklyn, New York. Writings associated with this teaching include all Watchtower publications, the Bible (New World Translation only), *Reasoning from the Scriptures*, *You Can Live Forever in Paradise on Earth*, *Watchtower* magazine, and *Awake!* magazine. Jehovah's Witnesses believe there is a one-person God (called Jehovah), no trinity. They believe that Jesus is not God, and before He lived on earth, He was Michael, the archangel. Jesus died on a stake (not a cross), and although His spirit was resurrected, His body was destroyed. Jesus is not coming again, though He did "return" invisibly in spirit in 1914. Salvation occurs through being baptized as a Jehovah's Witness and earning your way in through "door-to-door" work. Salvation in heaven is limited to 144,000 "anointed ones." These 144,000 live as spirits in heaven; the rest of the righteous (the great crowd) live on earth, and must obey perfectly for a thousand years or be annihilated. They do not observe holidays or birthdays, do not vote, do not serve in the military, salute the flag, or accept blood transfusions.

New Age Beliefs (Modern "Spirituality")

Scientology

Scientology was founded in 1954 by L. Ron Hubbard. The current headquarters are located in Los Angeles, California. The writings of this teaching are found in *Dianetics: The Modern Science of Mental Health* and others by Hubbard. Also used is *The Way to Happiness*. Those associated with Scientology do not define God or Supreme Being and generally reject the biblical description of God. Everyone is a "thetan," an immortal spirit with unlimited powers over its own universe, but not all are aware of this. Jesus is rarely mentioned in Scientology. Jesus was not the Creator nor an operating "thetan." He did not die for our sins. The Holy Spirit is not a part of this belief. Salvation is freedom from reincarnation; therefore there is no need to repent. One must work with his "auditor" on his "engrams" (hang-ups) to achieve the status of "clear," then progress up the "bridge to total freedom." Hell is a myth. People who get clear of engrams become operating thetans. Members observe the birth of Hubbard and anniversary publication of *Dianetics*.

Wicca

The roots of Wicca originate in nineteenth century Britain, partly inspired by Margaret Murray and organized by Gerald Gardner from the 1930s to the 1950s. This group does not have an official holy book, but uses *The Book of Shadows* by Gardner.

Also used is *A Witches' Bible* and The *Spiral Dance*. The supreme being is called the Goddess, which can be a symbol, the impersonal force of everything, or a personal being. Jesus is most often rejected altogether or considered a spiritual teacher who taught love and compassion. The Holy Sprit is not part of this belief; some believe "Spirit" can be referred to as a kind of divine energy. Ultimately, the Wiccans do not believe that humanity is sinful or needs saving. Importance is placed on honoring and working towards the preservation of nature (which they equate with the Goddess). Wiccans vary on the position of life after death (some are agnostic, some believe in reincarnation, and others believe in a wonderful place called Summerland). Wicca is an occultic "nature religion," not Satanism, and its adherents can be found casting spells, practicing rituals, and meeting for their eight major holidays.

World Religions

Judaism

The Jewish people have a special place in Christian history because we share the same beliefs of the Old Testament. Judaism began with Abraham of the Bible, about 2000 B.C., and Moses in the Middle East. Today, there are three main branches of Judaism—Orthodox, Conservative, and Reform—each with its own beliefs. The Holy Book of the Jewish faith is the Tanach (Old Testament), and the first fives books are collectively called the Torah.

There is no trinity belief in the Jewish faith; therefore Jesus is either seen as an extreme false messiah or a good martyred Jewish rabbi. Only the Messianic Jews and Hebrew Christians believe that Jesus was the Messiah and rose from the dead. Some believe that the Holy Sprit is God's activity here on earth—others say it's love and power. Many Jews believe prayer, repentance, and obeying the law are necessary for salvation. Others believe salvation is the improvement of society. Although some Jews do not believe in a conscious life after death, others believe there will be a physical resurrection. The Jewish people meet in synagogues on the Sabbath (Friday evening to Saturday evening) and honor many holy days and festivals. The holy city is considered Jerusalem.

Hinduism

The Hindu faith has no official founder, but its many different sects can be traced back to 1800-1000 B.C. in India. The many writings include the *Vedas*, the *Upanishads*, and the *Bhagavad-Gita*. According to Hindus, god is "The Absolute," a universal spirit. Everyone is part of God (Brahman), although most people are unaware of it. Hindus do not believe that Jesus rose from the dead or that His death atones for sin. Jesus is a teacher and son of God as are others. The Holy Spirit is not part of this belief. Salvation is released through cycles of reincarnation and achieved through yoga and mediation. This can take many lifetimes, and final salvation is absorption or union with Brahman. People can have reincarnation into a better status (good karma) if a person has behaved well. If he has been bad, a person can be reborn and pay for past sins (bad karma) by suffering. Some disciples wear orange robes and have shaved heads. Many Hindus worship stone and wooden idols in the temples.

Buddhism

Buddhism began with Gautama Siddhartha (563-483 B.C.) also known as Buddha ("Englightened One"). It was founded in modern-day Nepal as a reformation of Hinduism. Their teachings come from the *Mahavasstu* ("Great Story"), the *Jataka Tales*, the *Tripitaka*, and the *Tantras*. The Buddha himself did not believe in the existence of God. Jesus Christ is not part of the historic Buddhist worldview. Buddhists in the West today generally view Jesus as an enlightened teacher while Buddhists in Asia believe Jesus is an avatar or a *Bodhisattva* (but not God). The ultimate goal in life for a Buddhist is to achieve nirvana, to eliminate all desires or cravings, and in this way escape suffering. They use the Eightfold path as a system to be freed from desiring anything. This Eightfold path recommends right knowledge, speech, conduct, livelihood, right effort, mindfulness, and meditation as a way to this freedom. Salvation is achieved through reincarnation. Through the "Doctrine of Assimilation" other religions are blended into their form of Buddhism.

Islam (Muslims)

Islam was founded by Muhammad, who is the final "seal" of many prophets sent by Allah (God). The Islamic calendar began in A.D. 622, when Muhammad fled Mecca. The two main sects of the Muslim faith include Sunni and Shi'ite. The teachings of the Islamic faith come from the Qur'an (Koran) which was revealed to Muhammad by the angel Gabriel. The biblical Law of Moses, psalms of David, and gospel of Jesus (the *Injil*) are accepted in the Qur'an, but Muslim scholars teach that the Jews and Christians have corrupted these original revelations. Muslims believe that God (Allah) is One. The greatest sin in Islam is *shirk*, or associating anything with God. Many Muslims think that Christians believe in three gods, therefore are guilty of shirk. Jesus is one of the most respected of over 124,000 prophets sent by Allah. Jesus is not God and God is not Jesus. He was born of a virgin, but not crucified. Jesus, not Muhammad, will return one day for judgment—perhaps turning Christians to Islam. Under Islamic teaching, humans are basically good, but they are fallible and need guidance. The balance between good and bad deeds determines eternal destiny in paradise or hell. Fear of eternal torment is a prevalent theme of the Qur'an. Paradise includes a garden populated with *houris*, maidens designed by Allah to provide sexual pleasure to righteous men. Muslims (Islamic followers) go to mosque for prayer, sermons, and counsel. They make great efforts to spread Islam (*Jihad*). The five pillars of

Islam include: confess that Allah is the one true God and that Muhammad is the prophet, pray five times daily facing Mecca, give alms (money), fast during the month of Ramadan, and make a pilgrimage to Mecca once in a lifetime.

The Truth

> But, of course, being a Christian does mean thinking that where Christianity differs from other religions, Christianity is right and they are wrong. As in arithmetic —there is only one right answer to a sum, and all the other answers are wrong: but some of the wrong answers are much nearer being right than others.[63]
>
> —C.S. Lewis

Christianity

Christianity began with Jesus Christ and was founded in A.D. 30-33 under the Roman Empire. Followers of Jesus Christ became known as Christians. The key writing for our faith is in the Bible. As Christians, we believe that God is triune (three persons in one) as Father, Son, and Holy Spirit. God is a spiritual being without a body, and is personal and involved with people. He created the universe out of nothing. He is eternal, changeless, holy, loving, and perfect. Jesus is God; He has always existed and was never created. He is fully God and fully man. In becoming man, He was born of the virgin Mary. Jesus is the only way to the Father, salvation, and eternal life. He died on a cross according to God's plan, as a full sacrifice and payment for our sins. He rose from the dead on the third day, spiritually and physically immortal. For the next forty days he was seen by more than five hundred eyewitnesses. He ate meals and people touched His wounds. He physically ascended into heaven. Jesus will come again visibly and physically at the end of the world to establish God's kingdom and to judge the world. The Holy Spirit is God. The Holy Spirit is a person, not a force or energy field. He comforts, grieves, reproves, convicts, guides, teaches, and fills Christians. He is not the Father, nor is He the Son, Jesus Christ. Salvation is by God's grace, not by good works. Salvation must be received by faith. People must believe in their hearts that Jesus died for their sins and physically rose again, which is the assurance of forgiveness and resurrection of the body. This is God's loving plan to forgive sinful people. After death, believers go to be with Jesus and all people await the final judgment. Both saved and lost people will be resurrected. Those who are saved will live with Jesus in heaven. Those who are lost will suffer the torment of eternal separation from God (hell). Christians attend group worship, usually on Sundays in churches. There are no secret rites. Ultimately, Christians believe that Jesus is the Jewish Messiah promised to Israel in the Old Testament (Tanakh). Jesus said His followers would be known for their love for one another.

The most important decision you will ever make in life is where you put your faith. It's more important than where you go to college or whom you marry. Where is your faith right now? Are you depending upon what your grandparents believe? Are you depending on the fact that you go to church to show what you believe? Or have you made a personal inward decision to follow Jesus Christ and put your faith completely in Him? The Bible says "for all have sinned and fall short of the glory of God" (Romans 3:23). It also says, "Believe in the Lord Jesus Christ, and you will be saved" (Acts 16:31). The Bible goes on to reveal "that if you confess with your mouth, 'Jesus is Lord,' and believe in your heart God raised Him from the dead, you will be saved" (Romans 10:9). Making a decision to follow Christ is the greatest decision you will ever make in your life. If this issue has not been settled for you, or you have kept putting it off...there is no better time than now. All the other areas of your life will be out of balance and meaningless unless Christ is in the center of it. I challenge you and encourage you to give your life completely over to God before you go to college. He will guide you, direct you, and provide a supernatural peace in the process. Don't let the day escape you without taking a true inventory of where your faith is and how it will be affected during this next phase of your life.

Chapter Eleven Reflection Questions

1. What do you believe about God?

2. Why do you believe what you believe?

3. Do you have a personal relationship with Jesus Christ?

4. Have you studied other religions and religious sects such as Buddism, Hinduism, Islam, Mormonism, Jehovah's Witnesses, and even Judaism? If so, give a brief overview about what you have learned about them.

5. Have you ever wondered why you go to the Presbyterian church when your friends go to the Methodist, Baptist, Catholic, Lutheran, Episcopalian, Assemblies of God, Bible church, or other denomination of churches?

6. Are you prepared to tell others about why you believe what you believe? What is your testimony of how you came to know Jesus Christ as your personal Lord and Savior?

7. Which group are you going to fall into: the group that questions if there even is a God, or the group that pursues Him wholeheartedly during college?

Digging Deeper

■ Apologetics–Defending your faith using Scripture, logic, reason, and historical evidence. Answer the following questions according to what Scripture says in each situation.

- Is there really a God? Romans 1:20

- If God is good, why is there evil? Romans 8:22

- Is Christianity (Christ) the only way to heaven? John 14:6

- Is Jesus truly the Messiah predicted in the Old Testament? Isaiah 53 and John 7:28

- Is the Bible really inspired by God or written by men? 2 Timothy 3:16

- Is the Bible still relevant to today's culture? 1 Peter 1:24-25

■ Read what these scriptures say that warn against tapping into false spirits, cults, or religions:

- "Have nothing to do with _____ _____ and _____ _____ _____, rather train yourselves to be godly." 1 Timothy 4:7

- "See to it that no one takes you _____ through hollow and deceptive _____ which depends on human tradition and the basic principles of this world rather than on _____." Colossians 2:8

- "And do not let your people practice _____ _____, or use _____, or interpret _____, or engage in _____, or cast _____ or function as mediums or _____, or call forth the spirits of the _____. Anyone who does these things is _____ to our Lord. Deuteronomy 18:10-12 (NLT)

■ Choosing to follow Christ is the greatest decision you will make in your life. The "Romans Road" is a great tool to show you and anyone around you how to scripturally become a Christian:

- Romans 3:23

- Romans 6:23

- Romans 10:9

Chapter 12

. . . .

IS GOD A PART OF
YOUR VARSITY PLANNER?

All Scripture is God-breathed and is useful for
teaching, rebuking, correcting and training in
righteousness.

—2 Timothy 3:16

Have you ever known anyone who was training
for a marathon? The process is quite intense.
For months leading up to the official event
competitors record in a journal what they eat, log
when they workout, run various timed-trials, and
work their way up to practicing long runs every
week. Some even have toenails that fall off and
major bouts with diarrhea during training season,
but it doesn't stop their training. Why do they watch
their diet so meticulously, run so consistently every
day, and endure the pain that sometimes comes
alongside the process? For most, it's the satisfaction

of completing a challenging goal and crossing the finish line doing something they love. Others want that first-place trophy and love the competition of it all. How do I know? I had two roommates in college who ran up to twelve miles a day, and I watched this process again and again.

The pursuit of Christ can be described as a marathon (although not always as physically painful, thank goodness!). Of course, as Christians, we will never officially reach the "goal line" until we meet with Jesus face to face in heaven, but our life is a marathon-type journey of disciplining ourselves to set aside time to meet with Him, get to know Him, pray to Him, worship Him, and serve Him. And the true satisfaction is found in an inward peace that comes from a very real and personal relationship with our Lord and Savior. The apostle Paul uses this same analogy in 1 Corinthians 9:24-25: "Do you not know that in a race all the runners run, but only one gets the prize? Run in such a way as to get the prize. Everyone who competes in the games goes into strict training. They do it to get a crown that will not last; but we do it to get a crown that will last forever."

The word *discipline* isn't really popular in high school circles, but it's an important one, indeed, for growing in your faith so far from home in college. In light of the fact that your faith will be challenged and tested during these coming college years, there are things you can do to keep that close relationship with Christ. Many books, devotionals, and quiet time journals have been written to help guide us all in our daily Christian walk. What better time than in college to begin practicing the spiritual disciplines in a way that brings us that much closer to our Lord and Savior? One of my favorite books on these ideas is *Spiritual Disciplines for the Christian Life: The Study Guide* by Donald Whitney. He breaks these disciplines down into eight categories: Bible intake, prayer, worship, evangelism, serving, stewardship, fasting, and journaling.[64] I am no expert on any of these subjects, and I do not pretend to be disciplined in all these areas all the time. In fact, I remember when I was first exposed to all these different facets of the spiritual life and became genuinely overwhelmed. You may already be practicing all these disciplines (or just a few), but if not, don't be scared of them. They help provide a tremendous amount of success in achieving the abundant life that Jesus speaks of in the Gospel of John (John 10:10).

Bible Intake

In one of my favorite books about how to study the Bible called *Living by the Book* by Howard Hendricks, he opens with the line, "Shortly after I became a Christian, someone wrote in the flyleaf of my Bible these words: 'This book will keep you from sin, or sin will keep you from this book.'"[65] So true! God's Word is powerful, alive, relevant, and real. Hebrews 4:12 tells us, "For the word of God is living and active. Sharper than any double-edged sword, it penetrates even to dividing soul and spirit, joints and marrow; it judges the thoughts and attitudes of the heart."

It is God's map for us here on earth on how to get where *He* wants us to go in life. Warren and Ruth Meyers, authors of *Discovering God's Will*, paint a great picture of this idea,

> In His written Word, God has revealed His general will for all of us. Like an owner's manual for a new car, the Bible is our instruction Book, our operating manual from the One who made us. It gives us the principles and the do's and don'ts that we need if we want to keep our lives running well. We are never to seek further guidance on something that God has already commanded or forbidden in His Word! What He has said is enough.[66]

Studying the Bible can be confusing and overwhelming at times, but it's a lifelong journey. Some people like to study the Bible book by book, or by reading a couple of verses or chapters a day (having a Bible with commentary at the bottom is very helpful when doing this). Others like to have a devotional book guide them through Scripture and then provide some explanation. Some folks enjoy camping out in one book of the Bible for a while, dissecting verses, learning the history of the context, and looking up the original Greek and Hebrew meanings of words. Any way you do it, God can speak to you and begin to unveil truth to you in a way that no one else can.

A preacher once said that prayer is how we talk to God, and His Word is how He talks to us.

It's also the way we protect ourselves from our enemies. In Ephesians 6:11, Paul charges us to, "Put on the full armor of God so that you can take your stand against the devil's evil schemes." A few verses later, he describes this unique armor. The only offensive piece is the sword, which represents God's Word. Knowing the Word of God is the ultimate power we have against our enemy.

Prayer

Christian author Phillip Yancey preached at my church as a guest speaker, and his sermon was on the topic of prayer. In his opening remarks, he used a little humor to get the morning started. He talked about one major difference between men and women. He explained that men usually hold their feelings inside and rarely tell people what's really going on. Then he compared that with the venting that women often do in teacher's lounges, break rooms, and beauty parlors—deciding that really what they're doing rhymes with "witching." After some chuckles, he went on to explain that God longs for us to vent to Him…that the psalms are full of those intense feelings about life. Prayer is our chance to cry out to God how we really feel. It's also our chance to confess our sins and find freedom in His forgiveness. Even greater is the opportunity to come and intercede for others who may be in need or in trouble.

In any relationship (family, friend, or significant other) one must spend time with the other in order for that relationship to work. Even though God created you and knows everything about you, He still wants you to talk to Him so He can hear it all from you. I think of it this way. Every time I call my aging grandparents, they have already heard my updates, stories, and news (usually through my parents, who keep them posted on everybody). But they still love it when I call and give them the details from my perspective, my point of view, and hear it from my voice. We might not see each other often, but those phone calls I make represent the relationship I have with them.

Most importantly, we are to pray because Jesus prayed and left us with a model of how to do it through the Lord's prayer in Matthew 6:9-14. A simple acronym that helps me pray is **ACTS** (adoration of who God is, confession of things I've done, thanks for what God is doing, and supplication for others). Prayer is more for our benefit than God's, and don't we all have so much inside we want to get out? Author Stormie Omartian puts it this way:

> God wants you to long for *His* presence. He wants you to find your fulfillment in *Him* and nothing else. He wants you to walk closely with *Him*. He wants you to increase in faith and knowledge of *His* Word. He wants you to put all your hopes and dreams in *His* hands and look to *Him* to meet all of your needs. When you do, *He* will open the storehouse of blessing upon your life. That's

because these things are *His* will for you. But none of this happens without prayer.[67]

After all, like Becky Trabassi states in her book *Let Prayer Change your Life*, "Has not prayer been the means to escort a sinner through the gates of salvation and eternal life?"[68] Prayer really can change everything.

Worship

The definition of worship in my Bible is to express praise and devotion. When we worship God, we are acknowledging that He is the almighty, one, true God and that we adore Him and thank Him for all that He is. When I think of worship, I am reminded of the verse in Psalm 95:6, "Come, let us bow down in worship, let us kneel before the Lord our Maker; for he is our God and we are the people of his pasture, the flock under his care."

Worship is often synonymous with a "service" or a night of singing. We definitely can and should worship through songs, but worship takes on even more forms. We can worship with our lives. Donald Whitney describes worship as this: "Worship—focusing on and responding to God—is the duty and privilege of all people. Worship often includes words and actions but goes beyond them to the focus of our hearts and minds." He then goes on to say, "People become like their focus."[69] Worship is when our focus is on God alone—not ourselves, or other people, or things of this world. When we honor Him with our thoughts, actions, and words, He delights in us greatly.

Stewardship

My husband defines stewardship as how we spend our time, talents, and treasure. Usually when preachers teach on stewardship, the focus is on the treasure—or financial—aspect of our lives. All three are given to us by God, and He expects us to use them all wisely. How you spend your time, how you use your talents, and the way you handle your treasures are of utmost interest to our Lord.

College can be a dangerous time if those three aspects are not in check. When it comes to your time and talent, many opportunities will be provided for you to join various organizations, get involved in student government, or even become involved in a political campaign during an election year. Ann, a recent college graduate, credits her great use of her time and talent in college to keeping it simple. Carefully pick and choose those places that will receive your time and talent. Do them, and do them well, but don't worry about loading up your schedule with so many things that you wear yourself thin.

When it comes to protecting your treasure, be prepared for the mounds of credit cards you will receive in the mail with your name on them, ready to use. These credit card companies are hoping and wanting you to get so far into debt during your college years that you have to spend the rest of your life paying it off with incredible interest. If your family has set a certain budget for you, please respect and honor that. As we saw earlier, college itself is expensive. How you take care of the *little* God trusts you with now is a great indicator of how you will take care of *a lot* down the road. I am reminded of the verse in Luke 12:48, "From everyone who has been given much, much will be demanded; and from the one who has been entrusted with much, much more will be asked." If you have been given the great treasure of the college experience, enjoy giving back to the Lord! I encourage you to begin practicing the biblical principal of tithing 10% from your monthly allowance. This is the beginning of good stewardship with your treasures...and He has so much in store if you are faithful!

Fasting

This discipline that Whitney speaks of is also discussed in Richard Foster's *Celebration of Discipline*. Foster writes, "In a culture where the landscape is dotted with shrines to the Golden Arches and an assortment of Pizza Temples, fasting seems out of place, out of step with the times. In fact, fasting has been in general disrepute both inside and outside the Church for many years."[70] Our society is so obsessed with satisfied appetites that we often forget that we are most satisfied when we are close to our Lord. Fasting, as Jesus did in Luke 4:2, isn't just a spiritual excuse to lose weight, detox, or cleanse our systems (although it can do all these things). Skipping a meal or meals and substituting spiritual nourishment for physical nourishment is meant to help us grow in our relationship with the Lord. It should be God centered and God ordained.

Foster goes on to write that the "Who's Who" leaders of our faith in Scripture, which include Moses, David, Elijah, Esther, Daniel, Paul, and Jesus Himself, participated in fasting. Alongside them several great Christian leaders, such as Martin Luther, John Calvin, John Knox, John Wesley, and Jonathan Edwards also experienced the value of fasting.[66] That's reason enough to believe that fasting is a discipline that God desires for us to acquire— only that we may know Him more and be used for His kingdom.

Journaling

This final spiritual discipline is one that became my favorite during my college years. For high school graduation, a dear family friend gave me a journal with my name monogrammed in gold in the bottom right-hand corner. Starting that summer, I began journaling the scripture I read, thoughts I had, and prayers I prayed. Some were long, some were short, and some days were skipped, but how fun it is all these years later to go back and see what I was learning. On one special page, I wrote out things that I prayed God would give me in a husband one day. Nearly all of them came to fruition a decade later.

Journaling can be considered a continuous record of what God is teaching you. It is a great tool to track the "spiritual markers" in our growth as Christians similar to the spiritual marker stones the Israelites used in the book of Joshua (4:1-7) to be reminded of how God is faithful. The authors of the *Experiencing God* Bible study describe the idea of spiritual markers best:

> When Israel crossed the Jordan River into the promised land, God gave Joshua the following instructions: "Choose twelve men from among the people, one from each tribe, and tell them to take up twelve stones from the middle of the Jordan from right where the priests stood and to carry them over with you and put them down at the place where you stay tonight" (Josh. 4:2-3). These stones were to serve as a sign to the Israelites. Joshua explained, "In the future, when your children ask you, 'What do these stones mean?' tell them that the flow of the Jordan was cut off before the ark of the covenant of the lord. When it crossed the Jordan, the waters of the Jordan were cut off. These stones are to be a memorial to the people of Israel forever" (Josh. 4:6-7). The stones were to remind the people of a mighty act of God on their behalf. On many other occasions people built altars or set up stones as a reminder of significant encounters with God.[71]

Serving and Evangelism

Jesus came to earth to serve others in order to bring them to salvation. Serving and evangelism come in many forms, and it's exciting to discover ways that God wired you to bless and reach people for His kingdom. We'll discuss these two specific disciplines in detail later in another chapter.

The purpose of all these disciplines is to sustain, grow, and encourage your faith. Because Christ came, we are no longer bound to the Law, so do not let these rule over you in legalism. Instead, enjoy the blessings and freedom that come in growing in your Lord Jesus Christ. Our relationship with our Creator only deepens with the incorporation of these practices in our lives. Another of my favorite Tozer passages goes like this:

> Let us say it again: The universal Presence is a fact. God is here. The whole universe is alive with His life. And He is no strange or foreign God, but the familiar Father of our Lord Jesus Christ, whose love has for these thousands of years enfolded the sinful race of men. And always He is trying to get our attention, to reveal Himself to us, to communicate with us. We have within us the ability to know Him if we will but respond to His overtures. (And this we call pursuing God!) We will know Him in increasing degree as our receptivity becomes more perfect by faith and love and practice.[72]

I can't think of a better time than college to make these part of your everyday life! Our God wants you to know Him intimately, and that usually takes place through these practices. Don't be overwhelmed by trying to do them all at once. Start small, and then slowly add some as you feel comfortable. Remember, this is a marathon, not a sprint.

Chapter Twelve Reflection Questions

1. Which spiritual disciplines have you heard of and/or not heard of?

2. Which of the spiritual disciplines are you already in the habit of doing?

3. Which ones can you foresee being difficult for you to incorporate in your daily college routine?

4. Do any of these practices make you uneasy or confuse you?

5. Why would college be a good time to begin putting some of these spiritual disciplines into practice?

Digging Deeper

■   How do relationships generally work?

- Good (healthy) ones

- Bad (unhealthy) ones

- Is your relationship with God healthy or unhealthy?

■ Is it possible to know a lot *about* God, but not really *know* God?

- John 5:37-44
- Matthew 7:21-23

■ How can you *know* if you have a real relationship with God?

- John 14:21_____
- John 8:47_____
- John 15:5-8 _____

■ Where are you in your walk with Christ?
- Read Luke 8:4-15. Are you…

    ▪ Like the one who hears the Word, but then dismisses it and doesn't believe?
    ▪ Like the one who receives the Word with joy, but in time it falls away?
    ▪ Like the one who represents those who hear, but then is distracted by material things, life's worries, or having more fun?
    ▪ Like the one who represents those with a noble and good heart, who hears the

Word, retains it, and perseveres and produces a crop?

- Our walk with Christ can be compared to a
_____.

  - 1 Corinthians 9:24-25

■ Write down your thoughts as you read scripture concerning each of the following eight spiritual disciplines described by Donald Whitney in *Spiritual Disciplines for the Christian Life:*

- Daily Bible intake–Hebrews 4:12

- Prayer–Philippians 4:6

- Worship–Psalm 95:6-7

- Stewardship–Luke 12:48b

- Fasting–Acts 14:23

- Journaling–Joshua 4:1-7

- Serving–1 Corinthians 4:1

- Evangelism–Mark 16:15

∙ ∙

Chapter 13

SUNDAYS:
SLEEP IN OR SUIT UP?

As iron sharpens iron, so one man sharpens
another.

—Proverbs 27:17

Jen groaned when her alarm went off on her first
Sunday morning on campus. She had stayed
up until 3 A.M. talking and laughing with her
roommate, Paige, and the two girls next door, after
closing down the campus coffee shop at 1 A.M., where
Jen and Paige had run into a guy in Paige's history
class and his two friends.

Now the alarm was telling Jen it was time to get
up and get dressed for church, one she had picked
out before even arriving on campus because she had
heard about its great music and college group. *Maybe
I'll skip this one week because I'm so tired. I can't be*

exhausted for my classes tomorrow, she thought. *But I never miss church at home unless I'm sick.*

Jen hit the snooze button on her alarm and decided she'd figure it out after just five more minutes of sleep. She was facing her first "sleep in or suit up" challenge that this transition from home to college would throw her way.

You are probably too young to remember this sitcom, but in the eighties, a television show *Cheers* became wildly popular. The show centered around a handful of misfits from all walks of life coming to a bar named Cheers each afternoon to find comfort and community with somebody, anybody. Even the song for the introduction to the show said, "Sometimes you want to go where everybody knows your name…. And they're always glad you came. You want to go where you can see, troubles are just the same. You want to go where everybody knows your name."

This need for community is in all of us—not just those who hang out in bars. It is especially important for Christians to find comfort in one another through community. The authors of *Building Community* define it as this: "A Christian community is a small group of persons who come together on a regular basis to foster their spiritual, personal, and/or apostolic growth."[73] The same authors present great evidence that in the midst of a society that prides itself on individualism and pursues a change in the traditional family and social life…community is being highly sought out. God knew that His children needed each other in this tough world, so He structured the church to fill this need. Community has a variety of definitions, and hopefully this is a glimpse of the many places you will be able to find a Christian community to connect with during your college experience.

Finding a Church

During your senior year, you should have a chance to visit the campuses of your top college choices. One major recommendation I have for you during those college visits is to attend a church in the area with your family.

Attending with your family first can make it easier than walking in cold turkey by yourself. As you choose your college, get acquainted with your college town and meet some folks, you will find others who want to go with you. You don't need to feel pressure to *join* a new church, but getting connected to a church body is a biblical concept to help us grow in the Christian faith with others. In his article "Finding a Church," Kelvin Smith offers some great tips for finding your new church home:

- Find a church that preaches and practices the Bible.
- Look for an open and warm congregation.
- Meet with a pastor.
- Beware of a congregation whose membership is predominately students. (A mix of all ages

and stages of life usually represents a more balanced church body.)

- Make a commitment (after "church shopping" and finding the right fit for you).
- Look for chances to participate and plug in.[74]

Most college towns warmly welcome students and want them to be a part of Sunday school, Bible studies, retreats, and everything else they have to offer. The praise team at the church I attended throughout college was primarily college students. Many service projects and retreats were full of college students.

There is no substitute for finding a church home in a new city. Taking the time to get up and get dressed on Sundays can recharge your spiritual battery, challenge your walk, and ultimately connect you with other believers on your campus. I encourage you to make this your number one priority as you visit colleges and get settled in your new college town.

Christian-Based Organizations

There are other ways to connect with a Christian community, along with a church body, during your college years (that should not necessarily replace, but rather supplement your church community). Many campuses now have thriving Christian sororities and fraternities with folks who love Jesus and want His will for their lives. This is one way to instantly meet other Christians if you are not interested in the traditional Greek scene. Most familiar are the denominational organizations such as the Baptist Collegiate Ministries, Catholic Student Centers, Reformed University Fellowship (Presbyterian), the Wesley Foundation (Methodist), and many more that offer a place for you to gather during the week to fellowship with like-minded believers. Steve Shadrack, a college minister, father of college age students, and writer for *Boundless* Webzine, has boldly identified his top ten college ministries to which he would confidently entrust his own children:

1. Baptist Collegiate Ministries
2. Campus Crusade for Christ
3. Campus Outreach
4. Chi Alpha
5. Coalition for Christian Outreach
6. Great Commission Ministries
7. Intervarsity Christian Fellowship
8. Navigators
9. Reformed University Fellowship
10. Victory Campus Ministries[75]

I strongly encourage you to find out what college ministries are available on your campus and plug in to at least one early during your first semester.

Christian Bible Studies and Conferences

At Texas A&M University, a weekly Tuesday night Bible study called Breakaway eventually had to move out of a local church and into the basketball arena to fit the thousands of students coming each week to sing praises and hear God's Word come alive. I encourage you to do your homework and find out where these types of corporate worship and teaching are held (it doesn't have to be as big) that get you spiritually fed and connected to other Christians.

Also, be on the lookout for Christian conferences and retreats you may be interested in attending during your Christmas and spring breaks. The Passion movement led by Louis Giglio began my freshman year of college and ignited a fire in many hearts and souls from my campus, including mine. Those four days were full of thought-provoking discussion groups and speakers, and introduced me to an entirely new kind of Christian music that I still love. My husband was greatly moved after attending the Urbana conference, a missions conference held every three years. These intense days of worship and study also allow you to connect with believers on other campuses.

Finally, this is a great time to connect to small group Bible studies if you haven't been a part of those yet. Great Bible studies I recommend include anything by Henry Blackaby, Tommy Nelson, Beth Moore, Kay Arthur, Priscilla Shirer, or the Women of Faith series, just to name a few. These Bible studies can be done with a group in your church, your Christian fellowship groups, or with friends you meet around campus. A Bible study like this started

SUNDAYS: SLEEP IN OR SUIT UP?

with a group of students in our chemistry lab and turned out to be blast!

Christian Discipleship

The most intimate Christian connection is that of a one-on-one relationship. "One-on-ones" have become a popular and regular event with my grandfather when the family goes to visit. He enjoys having our individual, full attention so that he can ask the hard questions and give his opinions and advice back without distraction or interruption. This is exactly the environment created when Christians get together and share the honest truth about what's going on in each other's lives. In this kind of Christian community, a trustworthy space is created that allows both parties to get real with each other. Having real-life people serving as your figurative Paul, Barnabas, and Timothy found in Scripture allows you to see your life from another Christian perspective and keeps you accountable on the tough life issues.

Your "Paul" serves as a mentor in your life. This is typically someone who is a little further along in the faith, who has been there, made wise decisions, and wants to pour into you. In college, your Paul can be a godly professor you meet and want to spend time with, a Sunday school teacher you really connect with, an older student you admire, or anyone in the faith whom you see loves the Lord and is wise for his or her years. She can be a great neutral sounding board when you wrestle with changing your major, when dating issues arise, and simply to be there to guide you in your walk with Christ.

Your "Barnabas" serves as your biggest Christian cheerleader or friend and confidante who is walking alongside you in your world. She is usually a friend who has a strong faith who serves an encourager to you in your walk with Christ. She makes a great prayer partner as you share the ups and downs of your life with each other. Your "Barnabas" can be a sorority sister, a friend in your major, or even your roommate. These are the kinds of friends who cry when you cry, laugh when you laugh, and jump for joy when great things happen to you.

Your "Timothy" is someone you can pour into. In this relationship, you are the one further along in the faith with the wisdom to impart. You are a "Paul" to this person, serving as a sounding board and listening ear. You are the one asking the tough questions and keeping them accountable in their walk with Christ. A "Timothy" can be a high schooler in a youth group at your church, a new Christian you have met who is searching for more, or anyone you feel like God is calling you to pour into for a time. There is no greater purpose in a person's life than to disciple someone in Truth—and you will learn more than he or she will in the process.

All three aspects of this intimate discipleship setting will sharpen, challenge, and increase your faith. Pursuing deeper relationships such as these are sure-fire ways to keep from camping out in the gray areas during college.

Christian Music and Events

One huge bonus for Christians on campuses these days is the number of Christian musicians on the rise. These groups host worship in apartments, play at local coffeehouses, and even provide entertainment at social functions. A great resource for finding independent-label Christian music is independentbands.com. Maybe you yourself are talented musically. Don't be afraid to get involved in and even initiate Christian community on your campus through great music. It's fun, and it's a great way to grow in the faith.

Connecting with the body of Christ is not only our calling as Christians, it is essential in our growth as believers. Consider this quote by author Steven Garber:

> If understanding how belief becomes behavior is a result of a textured reading of the history of ideas, the ethic of character and the sociology of knowledge, then understanding those who have kept faith over the years —who with substantial integrity have connected belief to behavior, personally as well as publicly—requires the weaving together of three strands: convictions, character, and community.[76]

What better place to grow in conviction, character, and community, than with other believers during the most morally critical years of your life?

It's a good thing Jen finally rolled out of bed and eventually made her way to church that day. It just so happened to be "Welcome College Students" Sunday. At this annual after-church lunch in the gymnasium, all college students are given the opportunity to meet the pastors, learn about the opportunities to get involved, and ask questions to student leaders involved in the college Sunday school. At this very lunch, Jen met two girls who became great lifelong friends. Jen, Paige, and the two girls from church eventually started a Bible study in their dorm that impacted the lives of many freshmen and sophomores on campus. You just never know!

Chapter Thirteen Reflection Questions

1. Are you currently a part of a Christian community?

2. Why is it important as a believer to seek out and be involved in a Christian community?

3. Of the options listed in this chapter, which types of Christian community are most appealing to you?

4. Do you currently have a Paul, Barnabas, and Timothy in your life? If not, have you begun to pray that God would put people in your college path to help challenge, nurture, and encourage you in your faith?

5. What kind of community would you be bold enough to initiate if those around you had similar interests?

Digging Deeper

■ What is your definition of community?

■ Where do most people in life go to be encouraged and uplifted?

■ What do these scriptures say about the importance and purpose of Christian community?

   • Proverbs 27:17

   • Hebrews 10:24-25

   • Acts 2:42-47

Chapter 14

• •

ARE YOU
A MOLDY SPONGE?

So then, men ought to regard us as servants of
Christ and as those entrusted with the secret
things of God.

—1 Corinthians 4:1

The eighth-grader nailed it. Trying to conceptu-
alize the Christian life in a small group session,
she finally blurted out, "It's like a sponge.
Sometimes you're getting filled and sometimes you're
pouring out." I can't think of a theology book on the
shelf that says it better. And she's right. We connect
with God to get filled up, and then connect with
people to pour out. The only problem is…there are
lots of moldy sponges out there who constantly get
filled, but forget to pour back out.

As Mark 12:30 states, the greatest commandment
is to "Love the Lord your God with all your heart

and with all your soul and with all your mind and with all your strength." People sometimes leave out that second part, which commands us to "love your neighbor as yourself." After loving God, the next thing we are called to do is love people. This means everyone. This means family, friends, roommates, enemies, foes, and even those who disagree politically with us. The best way we can love people is by serving them and sharing with them the good news of Jesus Christ.

Wait a minute. Can the word "serve" and the word "college" really go together in the same sentence? Ask Joe White, owner and president of Kanakuk Kamps in Branson, Missouri, and I bet his answer would be an emphatic YES! Each summer over 2,500 Christian college students give up their summers of play, travel, and study to serve as counselors to kids and teenagers of all ages at each of their unique Christian campsites. Camp Ozark, Pine Cove Camps, and many others also offer this summertime experience that is challenging and rewarding in the area of serving. This is just one of many ways you could use your college time to make a difference and serve others.

Let's now take a closer look at the last two of the spiritual disciplines discussed in chapter twelve that have potential of great development during your college years.

Serving and Using Your Spiritual Gifts

Serving can sound like a scary word. I used to think it meant doing something really uncomfortable with people I didn't really know, to check off a "good deed for the day" on my really long to-do list. There are so many things that range from small minutes in your day to devoted hours during the week according to your schedule that you could do in order to serve Christ to those living around you, those in your church, or those on your campus.

The first thing most churches recommend when you want to get involved somewhere but don't know where is to take a spiritual gift test. As believers, God blesses us with special gifts that are to be used to edify the church and further the kingdom of Christ. This biblical principle is a great indicator of things you would most likely enjoy doing in any ministry venue. First Corinthians 7:7 reveals that all believers are given at least one gift, and 1 Timothy 4:4 commands us not to neglect these gifts which are imparted to us to edify the church and further the kingdom of Christ. First Corinthians 12 gives great detail concerning the types of gifts believers may receive, and also how they work together in the body of Christ. The following list highlights the most common forms of spiritual gifts found in believers:[77]

- Administration/ruling
- Craftsmanship
- Discernment

- Evangelism
- Apostleship/pioneering
- Creative communication
- Encouraging
- Faith
- Giving
- Hospitality
- Interpretation
- Leadership
- Healing
- Intercession
- Knowledge
- Mercy
- Miracles
- Prophecy
- Teaching
- Wisdom
- Shepherding
- Serving
- Tongues

If you haven't already, take time to discover your gifts (these inventory tests can be picked up at most churches) and begin taking a stab at putting them into practice. It may take awhile to find your niche in a church or in a ministry setting, but the fun is found in the journey. During your college years, you will be blessed with the gift of time. Make the most of it by developing the gifts God has given you to impact His kingdom!

When I think of serving and putting spiritual gifts to their best use, I can't help but think of one of my college roommates, and now best friend, who gave endlessly of herself during her college years. As busy as she was as a full-time student, chaplain of her sorority, and working part-time at the school newspaper, she single-handedly started a prison ministry at a local juvenile detention center in our college town through the support of the church we attended. Each week she organized Bible study groups and leaders to go and sing to and share the gospel with those troubled kids. I knew it was prison day when I could smell the brownies in the oven—she always brought sweets and treats for the delinquent boys. Talk about a servant!

Others were Young Life leaders in secondary public schools, tutors for the athletic community, and involved in various charity groups on campus such as United Way, Boys and Girls Clubs, Big Brother Organizations, and Adopt a Street. Some served through working at local women's shelters. Others served in church choirs and church-initiated organizations as well as mission trips led by church ministries during summer, winter, and spring breaks.

However, service does not always come in the form of an organized group. Serving can come in the way of picking up someone without a car and driving him or her to campus, stopping traffic if a fellow biker has had an accident on campus, cleaning the dorm room bathroom for the hundredth time without complaining, or simply inviting your difficult roommate to a Christian event with you.

Evangelism

Evangelism is another spiritual discipline (and sometimes scary word) that can really take off during your college years. We might not all have evangelism as our vocation as the great Billy Graham does, but we can each be prepared for those interested, reluctant, or new to the idea of Christianity. Earlier we talked about knowing what you believe and why you believe it, and I encourage you, as Paul writes in his letters to the Colossians, to be ready to share the gospel when the timing is right.

Along the same lines of the spiritual gift test is an evangelism style indicator you can test yourself on to see which style you are most comfortable using to share the gospel. In his book *Becoming a Contagious Christian*, Bill Hybels walks his readers through different evangelism styles found throughout the Bible, such as Peter's confrontational approach, Paul's intellectual approach, the blind man's testimonial approach, Matthew's interpersonal approach, and the Samaritan woman's invitational approach.[78] How exciting it is to know that God created you with a story to tell in a way you feel comfortable telling it! Don't be afraid to start sharing your faith on your campus.

I am reminded that Jesus came to earth to serve, love, and show us the way to salvation. In many of these venues of service, lots of folks come to know the Lord. Service and evangelism take a proactive effort and sometimes—not always—go hand in hand. Being available to put others as a priority and being ready to share your faith at a moment's notice is something God wants and calls us to be ready for. What better time to start putting those disciplines in practice than when your only responsibility in life is yourself.

Chapter Fourteen Reflection Questions

1. What comes to mind when you think of the word *serve*?

2. Would you be interested in taking a spiritual gifts test to find out your gifting in order that you might enjoy serving Christ in some capacity?

3. Of the organizations and opportunities to serve listed earlier, what sparks your interest the most as far as a place to serve in your college town?

4. What do you think of when you think of the word *evangelism*?

5. Would you be interested in reading about the different evangelism styles in order to find out which ones you connect with most?

Digging Deeper

■ Can the word *serve* and the word *college* go in the same sentence?

- Mark 12:31
- 1 Corinthians 4:1
- Galatians 5:13

■ Ministry is messy, but the rewards are life-changing!

- Philippians 2:17
- Ephesians 3:20

■ What can I do and where do I start?
- Figure out your spiritual gifts.
  - 1 Corinthians 7:7
  - 1 Timothy 4:4
  - 1 Corinthians chapter 12

- Talk to someone in your church about ways your gifts could be used.

PART FOUR
GROWING IN
THE SOCIAL LIFE

And Jesus grew in wisdom and stature, and *in favor with* God and *men*.

—Luke 2:52

P erhaps the most anticipated part of college is the people part. With whom will I live? Will I make any friends? Will I survive sorority rush? Will I find my husband? You are not alone if these kinds of questions trump all other anxieties concerning your upcoming transition. The person you become in college will be directly related to the people with whom you choose to spend your time.

As stated earlier, when Christ grew in favor with man, this is not to imply that He *sought* the favor of men. Actually, it was just the opposite. He lived a life in front of people that was so radical, so attractive, and absolutely counter to the culture of that day that people were drawn to Him. Did He have friends? Yes! "Jesus chose twelve disciples, but He seemed especially close to three of them—Peter, James, and John—and even closer to just one—John, whom He called Beloved."[79]

Then He had the multitudes whom He healed, loved, and taught and who followed Him daily. He had a mom and a dad and a family. And because John 11:35 states that Jesus wept and Matthew 21:12 implies that He became angry, Christ was absolutely emotionally involved in lives.

Life is about knowing our God and making Him known to other people. With whom we surround ourselves can't help but play a huge role in who we become. Another favorite quote of mine from Steven Garber is:

> One thing I have learned is that it is the people you surround yourself with—that is one of the most important choices you make. I chose my employer. She hired me. But you have to serve somebody, and it's who you serve that is the choice. I choose my friends, and they do respond to my overtures and affections, but the people I surround myself with on a regular basis—even on an irregular basis—are people who in many ways are more than I am. That is absolutely essential, because they always cause me to go back and wonder what else I need to do. Do I guard my friends' reputations, do I care for my friends

in the way that they demonstrate so marvelously and consistently? The people I consider my wise counselors and the pillars of my life are people who in many ways are more than I am.[80]

What kind of friends are you going to attract and what kind of friend do you want to be? What kind of dating reputation will you build? When it comes to relationships and your future, give all your anxieties to the Lord. He already knows the end of your story. The Bible gives us such great boundaries when it comes to how to handle the many people in our lives. On the days of confusion, frustration, doubt, and fear, lean on this verse found in Psalm 37: 3-4: "Trust in the Lord and do good; dwell in the land and enjoy safe pasture. Delight yourself in the Lord and He will give you the desires of your heart." As long as you remember to worship the Creator and not the created, you'll be just fine.

Chapter 15

. . . .

LIVING WITH
A STRANGER

Be wise in the way you act toward outsiders;
make the most of every opportunity. Let your
conversation be always full of grace, seasoned
with salt, so that you may know how to answer
everyone.

—Colossians 4:5-6

'll never forget his advice. He was the guest speaker
talking about relationships at a youth event when
I was in high school. He told us to begin praying
right then for our future roommates in college and
our future mates we would someday marry. For
whatever reason, it stuck. Boy, was I glad I did.

For the many of you who did not share a room
with a sibling growing up, sharing a room with a
stranger can be one of the most difficult adjustments
when going off to college. An MIT Web site says it

best: "Negotiating the respect of personal property, personal space, sleep, and relaxation needs can be a complex task. The complexity increases when room-mates are of different ethnic/cultural backgrounds with very different values."[81] That last part hit home for me.

Remember Pratima, the roommate I mentioned in the faith chapter? Living with someone from a different country, who belonged to a different religion and approached life from a totally different perspective brought on a series of issues that made certain days more difficult than others. Obviously, God ordained this living situation…and that is the best way to approach the potluck roommate gamble. Some of my great friends from college met through the potluck lottery and hit it off from day one. Others had unique circumstances and needed a change, effective immediately. Some had the hum-drum relationships that were strictly living circumstances until the next year rolled around. In whichever situation you may find yourself, remember that God has a purpose and a plan for who your roommate is. Having prayed for mine for some time, and with our religious quizzing episode that started our first night, I had a hunch this one was definitely ordained. If I didn't believe it then, I believed it a few months later during another "Aha!" moment with Pratima.

One evening, I had been out studying late with some friends and strolled in around one or two in the morning. Not wanting to wake up Pratima, I sneaked in extra quietly, not turning on any lights or making any unnecessary noise. I thought about doing my devotion, but for some reason, sleep sounded so much better than turning on my nightstand lamp, scrambling for my Bible, and reading for another fifteen minutes. As soon as I was snuggled deep in my down comforter, I heard a soft voice from across the room clearly say to me, "You haven't spent time with your God today." With a cold chill shivering down my spine and completely shocked at the boldness of this girl, I sat straight up in bed and answered, "You know, you are right…I haven't."

I then rubbed my eyes and followed my usual nighttime devotion protocol. I don't remember the verse I read, the devotion topic, or what I prayed that night, but I do remember vividly seeing the purpose of my living with this girl named Pratima. She was not impressed with my spiritual knowledge or personal testimonies, but she watching my actions. Roommates, whether you want them to or not, will be watching your every move. Friend or foe, if you claim to be a follower of Jesus Christ, they will be the first to testify whether or not your actions match your words.

The good news is, not all roommate situations are quite that intense. Julia DeVillers, author of *The College Dorm Survival Guide*, gives great tag lines to potential roommate situations:

- The **Here-And-Now Roommate**–The kind you don't really hang out with, but both have a great mutual respect for each other. Probably won't talk much after college.

- **The Never-Again Roommate**–The kind where things start off rocky and end with an explosion. Unfortunately something happens that makes both parties never really want to talk again.

- **The-Right-Amount-Of-Distance-Roommate**– These folks usually don't have a ton in common but are very considerate of each other and each other's space. They each have their own lives, and sometimes after living together eventually become friends.

- **The Ex-Friends Roommate**–This happens when two or more friends from high school assume living together will make them even closer. For whatever reason, this does not happen and sometimes drives the friendship apart.

- **The "Lifers"**–This roommate situation happens when living together turns into becoming best friends. After college, the relationship continues and they become support systems for each other throughout life.[82]

During your first year of college, you will hopefully make many new friends. The next three years you'll buddy up with those you enjoy and rent apartments, live in the sorority house, or even live in a real house. Those relationships can be very interesting as you face cooking in a kitchen together for the first time, cleaning a toilet, and having to learn how to call the cable guy when it's acting haywire again. Here are a couple of things to think about, whether it's your freshman or senior year living with a roommate:

1. Try to make your bed every morning. For some reason, this always makes a space (especially as small as a dorm room) seem bigger and cleaner.

2. Designate certain shelves of the bathroom, mini-fridge, or pantry as "yours and hers." You will thank me later when you were craving that last bite of the cookies and cream ice cream...and it's still there.

3. For apartment living, keep the "community areas," such as the kitchen, living room, and dining area, free of your piles of clutter.

4. Rinse your dishes and put them in the dishwasher after each use. Discuss early on the cleaning routine and who is responsible for what.

5. Together, go buy a roll of stamps and split it down the middle for paying bills. Discuss the paying of the bills routine when you first move in.

6. Create a space for mail and messages. Possibly consider buying a white eraser board and cork board community message center to help keep everyone organized and on the same page.

7. Discuss openly and honestly your comfort level when it comes to alcohol in the room and boys sleeping over. Also consider discussing the routine if out of town company wants to stay in your dorm room or apartment.

8. Be careful not to leave personal ID numbers and passwords out for the world to see if you are sharing a computer.

9. Talk out things that are your pet peeves or medical issues during your first couple of days as roommates. Being open about the fact that you're allergic to peanuts or that you don't talk much in the morning will certainly help prevent a trip to the emergency room or an awkward conversation later on.

10. Don't think that you and your roommate always have to be together or be best friends. Enjoy each other, but enjoy having your own friends as well.

11. If it's not yours, don't touch it. This is especially important when you are tempted to rummage through your roommate's closet for the perfect date outfit. Most girls don't like sharing clothes. Always ask before you touch, take, or use anything that is not yours.

12. Have fun! Laugh at yourself and forgive others easily. Keeping things lighthearted will keep you from getting frustrated and becoming a gossip.

Living arrangements can sometimes make or break your college experience. Being prayerful, mindful, and respectful of the whole situation going into it can be your greatest asset entering this new adventure. Most colleges give you compatibility surveys, but as you can see...that doesn't always work out! And make sure you take those dirty dishes to the sink. Otherwise, you might find them tucked between your sheets and your comforter.

Chapter Fifteen Reflection Questions

1. Have you prayed for your future roommate?

2. What kind of person are you naturally...organized or cluttered?

3. Of the pointers given, which ones stand out as the most challenging to consider?

4. What is your plan if your roommate is self-destructive (e.g., into binge drinking, drugs, or considering suicide)?

5. What are some of your pet peeves that you will need to either clearly communicate or show a little grace on during these college years?

Digging Deeper

■ What do the following scriptures say about a potentially awkward "potluck" roommate situation?

- Colossians 4:5-6

- Philippians 2:3-5

■ Scriptures to help you be a better roommate:

- Don't _____ against each other. James 5:9

- Avoid godless _____. 2 Timothy 2:16

- Our _____ should be like Jesus. Philippians 2:5

- Guard your _____. Proverbs 13:3

- A _____ separates close friends. Proverbs 16:28

- Live out the _____ of the _____. Galatians 5:22

FRIENDS ARE FRIENDS FOREVER?

Perfume and incense bring joy to the heart, and the pleasantness of one's friend springs from his earnest counsel.

—Proverbs 27:9

When you go to college, you will be surrounded by people who don't know you," states Derek Melleby in his article "Navigating the College Transition."[83] And that can be a scary thing. All of a sudden, the people you meet won't know that your mom had a brain tumor when you were in the fourth grade, that you were Mary in the Christmas play for seven years straight, or that you were the only one not to make the cheerleading squad out of all your friends your junior year. On one hand, it can seem exhausting introducing yourself from scratch to everyone you meet. On the other hand it can be incredibly freeing to let go of any negative stigmas that scarred you in your hometown—all this in order to make friends.

It's a common fact that whom you surround yourself with in college will greatly affect your college experience. In the first of several studies led by the College Transition Project, one of the three biggest fears of going off to college was how to make friends.[84] This is much easier said than done, but it is a natural part of any college experience. Thank goodness every other freshman on campus is having the same questions, doubts, and fears about meeting people they will click with as you are. You are all in the same boat together. It's not like they have been doing the college thing for a while, and you're the new kid having to come in late and catch up. It's that freshman year when groups are forming and roommates connect roommates with other random people they met in the cafeteria, in line getting books, or in their first class.

Where Do I Meet People?

Attending your campus orientation week is the first place you will most likely find yourself meeting folks. Use this opportunity to take down cell phone numbers and e-mails of those you would like to reconnect with when school starts back up. Another great place to meet people is in the hall of your dorm when moving in. There is something about the chaos, the heat, and the lingering emotional parents that bond everyone together. This is also a great time to introduce yourself and ask if anyone would want to go to church with you. Other than church, another great place to meet people is at the club and organization booths during the first open house. There you will find people of all sorts sitting behind organizational booths that reveal right away the activities, hobbies, and even religion they prefer. And of course, there is sorority rush, which we will talk about in depth during the next chapter. For girls, this is the number one way to meet other like-minded girls. Standing in those alphabetical lines for hours and hours day after day for a whole week before school starts will definitely bond some of you for life. In fact, I met some of my dearest friends during that rush-week experience. Whether you think sorority life is for you or not, consider going through rush just for the sake of meeting people.

I want to take a few moments to address the idea of "Facebook" friendships. I have nothing against these new cyber social circles, but many college students have asked me to include that it cannot replace having *real* face time with friends. Sitting at a computer posting pictures, tagging friends, and downloading your favorite tunes to your personal page is not a real relationship with anyone. I highly encourage you to use this great tool as a means to keep up with folks, make plans, and stay updated on the latest happenings, but not as the basis for your friendships. This can also become a great time waster if you are not careful. Keep yourself in check with how much time you are spending on your Facebook page versus real face time with people.

Down the college road, you will find yourself joining campus organizations, organizing study groups, being assigned to group projects, and sitting in classes with people you start to recognize. Think about what you want in a friend and first try to be that. If you want Christian friends, you might have to dig deep…but they are there, I promise. Surround yourself with uplifting people who enjoy life, who want to be successful academically, and have the same values you do. Their encouragement and accountability will lift your spirits when you are down and catch you before you fall. Having a prayer partner, Bible study group, or friend who asks you hard questions is the key to not going off the deep end during those wonderful college days. Ask the Lord now to begin preparing not only a roommate, but a group of friends you connect with to help make your college years the most rewarding they can be.

Old Friends vs. New Friends

"It's interesting. You sign a contract for marriage, a license to drive a car, a mortgage to own a house, a W-4 form for a job, an agreement to join a health club, a birth certificate for your kids, but there are no documents to bind you to a friendship. No sealed stamp of commitment. No official guidelines… unless you consider God's Word."[85] This quote from the Women of Faith Bible Study Series, *Celebrating Friendship,* points out how our culture automatically sets up rules, boundaries, and contracts for almost every other type of relationship in life except the most basic one found in a friend! My favorite biblical examples of friendships are those of David and Jonathan found throughout the book of 1 Samuel, as well as the friendship of Mary and Elizabeth found in Luke 1. Thank goodness we have the Bible as a God-breathed guide on how this most wonderful and necessary relationship of life works.

As you may already know, another challenge for students attending college is keeping up with old friends while also wanting to make new ones. As touched on earlier, you probably fit into one of three categories when going off to school: you want to go to a school where you don't know anyone and want to "start over" completely; you want to go to your school of choice hoping that some folks you know will be going with you; or you and your circle of friends by chance ended up—or not by chance and decided—to attend the same college.

If you want to go to college to start over completely, then keeping up with old friends takes more effort on your part. Keeping up through Facebook postings, e-mails, chats on-line, and the occasional phone call usually keeps the friendship alive. Friendships from back home will seem long-distance and take a great effort to stay in touch, but enjoy all the perks of gaining a whole new social circle in your new setting.

If you are going to the school of your choice and have some hometown folks going with you, then keeping up won't be quite as difficult. Make time in your schedule to reconnect and hang out with old friends, and also make the effort to develop new friends. Often these circles collide, and your friend base just gets bigger and bigger without much effort. You will still have some friends back home or at other colleges with whom you will want to stay in touch.

Those of you going with your best friends (and possibly rooming with them) will have a more difficult time making new friends if you're not careful. Having an instant comfort zone follow you to college can be a wonderful thing, but it can also keep you from branching out. Obviously, keeping up with old friends won't be a problem for you, but make sure you are setting aside time for the new ones.

In all these cases, it can be a tough balance trying to find time for both the old and the new friendships. Once you get into the college groove, it's not really that difficult. College is the one time in life when everyone starts off on the same playing field. Enjoy it, and try not to stress about the rest.

Do You Want Christian Friends or Catty Friends in College?

Now let's talk about the new friends you are going to make in college. The Bible calls us to love everyone. But those whom you choose to invest in, spend time with, and share your deepest thoughts with will inevitably make an impression on you–and you on them. Just as you want to attract the right kind of person when dating, the same is true for making friends. Haley Dimarco, author of *Mean Girls All Grown Up*, says it like this,

> Girls are important. And as you get older, what you are doing when you surround yourself with women (and by that I mean you have at least three good girlfriends) is preparing yourself for the future. Men come and go, but if you keep your friendships strong, you will always have a shoulder to cry on.[86]

When it comes to making good friends, the old saying is true—to have a friend, you have to be one. Later in her *Mean Girls* book, Dimarco gives a great checklist to run through concerning your friends:

1. Is she overly defensive?
2. Does she love to talk about other people?
3. Does she love revenge?
4. Is she religious or spiritual?
5. Does she always have to look good?
6. Is it always about her?
7. Does she always flatter you?
8. Does she forgive?
9. Is she jealous of your wins?
10. Do you feel better or worse after spending time with her?[3]

Think about these questions on two levels. How would you respond to these questions concerning your friends? Then how would your friends answer them about you? When it comes to making friends and being a friend, consider *The Message* version of 1 Peter 3:8-9: "Summing up: Be agreeable, be sympathetic, be loving, be compassionate, be humble. That goes for all of you, no exceptions. No retaliation. No sharp-tongued sarcasm. Instead, bless—that's your job, to bless. You'll be a blessing and also get a blessing."

Finding and maintaining great friendships is also a lifelong journey. Some will come and go in seasons, and some will remain lifelong buds. Being the best friend you can be will most certainly help you attract and keep the right kind of friendships.

Homesickness and Depression

Everyone going to college experiences some level of sadness about being away from home, family, and close friends. Whether or not your friends go to college with you or you start over completely, expect a time (for me it was Sunday afternoons) when you wish you could click your red heels, whisper "There's no place like home," and just be home. J. Budziszewski puts it this way: "Whether lonely or not, everyone is affected somehow by alone-ness because we were designed to be with others. God said it wasn't good for Adam to be alone, and it isn't good for us either."[87] That is why it is critical to make efforts to find a great group of godly friends your first few weeks and months of college.

Don't get discouraged if you get homesick occasionally. And don't think you are crazy if you feel yourself in a "funk" every so often. Most colleges provide counselors on campus to help guide you through these types of issues and tough times if you ever need them. As easy as it would be to jump in your car or book a flight home every weekend you get lonely, try to avoid that temptation. Instead, use those moments as inspiration to pro-actively organize a social event for the weekend. Extend an invitation to those around you in class or in the dorm…you never know what might come of it. At the same time, recognize that there is a significant difference in the occasional homesick feeling and full-blown depression.

Depression can become a serious issue in college if not caught or treated early. According to Barrett Seaman, author of *Binge: What Your College Student Won't Tell You*, "Suicide is the second leading cause of death among North Americans of college age. It occurs at an annual rate of one per ten thousand nationwide."[88] That's serious. Keep yourself in check and watch out for others around you who concern you when in comes to the downward spiral of depression. If you do find yourself depressed often, continue to give your concerns to the Lord, talk to someone about how you are feeling, and get professional help. You are not alone in feeling lonely, I promise.

Having friends and being a good friend will hopefully prevent this terrible condition from consuming your college years. My prayer is that God will protect you from this common college battle and bless you with many great friends!

Chapter Sixteen Reflection Questions

1. What kind of friend are you currently?

2. Have you prayed for God to bring you Christian friends during your freshman year?

3. Where are some places you might feel comfortable introducing yourself to others?

4. Write down a list of things you enjoy doing or things that are important to you. This is probably the best place to start when finding people you click with.

5. What does Scripture say about whom you surround yourself with in life?

Digging Deeper

■ Being a godly friend: What the Bible says about being a good friend

- Proverbs 27:9 _____
- Hebrews 3:13 _____
- Hebrews 12:14 _____
- Proverbs 27:17 _____
- 1 Peter 3:8-9 _____
- Colossians 3:12-14 _____

■ Read about the friendship between David and Jonathan in 1 Samuel 19 and 20. What are qualities in that friendship worth emulating?

■ Read about the friendship between Mary and Elizabeth in Luke 1. What are qualities in that friendship worth emulating?

Chapter 17

. . . .

THE SCIENCE
BEHIND SORORITIES

Am I now trying to win the approval of men,
or of God? Or am I trying to please men? If I
were still trying to please men, I would not be a
servant of Christ.

—Galatians 1:10

Like it or not, there is a science behind the sorority system, and it can be a controversial topic
among many Christians. The behind-the-scenes
picking and choosing can put a knot in your stomach
and remind you of the days on the playground when
you were chosen last (or not at all) for kickball
during afternoon recess. In the previous chapter, I
made my case that for girls, at least, the sorority rush
experience is a great way to meet people. However,
I did not always hold this view. Disappointed in so
many girls from my hometown that came home with

all these crazy, wild sorority stories, I was convinced during my senior year of high school that I would not join one when I went to college. With a nudge from my mom and a few others, I finally concluded that I would go through the rush process solely for the purpose of meeting people.

If you haven't encountered it already, the process of going through rush takes an enormous amount of preparation. You have all these hometown Pan-Hellenic meetings conducted by overdressed women with really big hair giving you a to-do list longer than your English final. Then you have "recs" to collect, which for me meant interviews with women I didn't know, asking me questions I did not care anything about, to get into a sorority I had never heard of. To top it off, I had to get a certain outfit for each day—no thanks. Well, even if that sort of thing is not your cup of tea, take the time to do your homework. It may be annoying, and if your mom wasn't in a sorority, it may be extra difficult. But, if there is any inkling in you that you might enjoy it, do it. Rush week is most certainly a week of overwhelming fake smiles, how do you do's, and proper etiquette reminders, but it can be a great opportunity for you to find a group of girls you click with who will help make these college years extremely rewarding.

Maybe you are on the other end of the spectrum and are certain that you will get into your sorority of choice because of your triple legacy status (meaning your sister, mother, and grandmother all pledged the same sorority during their college days). The week-long experience (for some it's a whole semester when pledging is in the spring instead of fall) is a dramatic process of you cutting sororities and sororities cutting you. This can be painful if you are not aware of the process, and emotions can easily get wrapped up in this intense estrogen fest. Please don't let your security rest in the letters you want to wear across your chest. If you are banking on this experience to fill your college confidence tank, take another look in the mirror and remember who you are. What goes on behind the scenes of that rush week is so mysterious and fleeting, that having your security depend on one bid day will only bring you pain in the end. In *The Search for Significance*, Robert McGee calls people of this nature "approval addicts." He states, "Our self-concept is determined not only by how we view ourselves but by how we think others perceive us. Basing our self-worth on what we believe others think of us causes us to become addicted to their approval."[89] You are a child of God; the purpose of sororities is not to give you an identity. It can bring you a wonderful group of friends, but it cannot replace the most wonderful relationship with our Lord and Savior, Jesus Christ.

At the same time, sorority life is not for everyone. There will be alcohol readily available at almost every social function. There will be a series of weird things you have to do during your initiation period (although things have quieted considerably with hazing lawsuits in recent years), and you will see

COLLEGE BOUND ON SOLID GROUND

"wild" on a level you never dreamed possible. If you can stay true to your values, think of yourself as a witness for Christ, and surround yourself with like-minded girls within your pledge class and sorority, then you will be fine. If you are a follower who tends to go with the flow to be accepted, then think twice before going through rush. This is where the Christian "mixed-signal" idea can become magnified in your life if not careful. Sorority life can easily become a place where you play Christian on Sundays (even dressing up for lunch if you didn't make it to church), but live quite differently on Thursday, Friday, and Saturday night at the campus mixers and fraternity crush parties. Tozer speaks so well of the "double life" often seen in Christian lives—especially during the college years—when he eloquently writes:

> One of the great hindrances to internal peace which the Christian encounters is the common habit of dividing our lives into two areas—the sacred and the secular. As these areas are conceived to exist a part from each other and to be morally and spiritually incompatible, and as we are compelled by the necessities of living to be always crossing back and forth from the one to the other, our inner lives tend to break up so that we live a divided instead of fulfilled life.[90]

The college experience and life in a sorority do not give you permission to live a double life. Rather, we are called to invite Christ into all the areas of our lives. Taking a stand in any arena takes discipline, accountability, and a bold attitude. If these are not qualities that come easily to you, then think long and hard about whether or not you will fall under the temptations that sororities bring. On the other hand, if these qualities do come easily to you, be careful not to condemn and judge those who are not believers or who are new to the faith because that can be a hard reputation from which to recover. Girls from all backgrounds, hometowns, and faith perspectives will become your sorority project leader, your community service partner, or even your roommate in the sorority house. Know where you stand and don't move. Love all those around you, and still don't move. Your life and your actions speak much louder than your words. Francis of Assisi's famous quote still applies today: "Preach the gospel every day, and if you have to—use words."

Reasons You Might Enjoy Sorority Life as a Christian

- You meet lots of people quickly.
- You have instant events on your social calendar.
- You are surrounded by a range of personalities, many faiths (unless you are at a Christian college), and people at various places in their walks with Christ.
- The sorority house meals are some of the best in town!

- You have an instant network from which to pull later on when looking for a job.
- There are many philanthropic opportunities in which you can serve and volunteer.
- It is a great place to live out your faith and possibly bring people into the faith.
- It provides wonderful leadership and scholarship opportunities.
- Most sororities have grade requirements and mandatory study hours which keep you on track academically.
- You make friends that are lifelong.

For those of you who decide sorority life is something you are interested in, there is an unfamiliar language full of new terms and words you will soon encounter. As you get your recommendation packets ready (and turned in on time!), you may pick up on a few of these new vocabulary words. Here is a great list of "sorority lingo" definitions a friend shared that might help take off that anxious edge:

- **Active**–a fully initiated member of a fraternity or sorority.
- **Alumna/alumnus (alumni is the plural)**–a graduated member of a fraternity or sorority.
- **Bid**–a formal invitation to pledge a fraternity or sorority.
- **Chapter**–the local group of their larger national organization, designated by a special Greek letter name.

- **Formal rush**–a series of parties given by each fraternity or sorority during the fall rush period.
- **Fraternity**–a group of individuals bound together by ritual ties and common goals. Women's fraternities are often informally called sororities.
- **Greek**–a member of a fraternity or sorority.
- **Hazing**–forced or required activity that can be mental or physical and is strictly forbidden.
- **Initiation**–the formal introductory membership ceremony where the sorority's ritual is exposed to the pledge/associate and brings him/her into full membership.
- **Legacy**–a prospective member whose mother or sister was in the same sorority, or whose father or brother was in the same fraternity.
- **National Pan-Hellenic Council (NPC)**–the governing body of all sororities in North America.
- **Pin**–(two types) the *active pin* (or badge) is a distinctive insignia, worn on the chest, designating an active member of a particular sorority or fraternity; the *pledge pin* is an insignia used to designate a pledge/associate of a particular sorority or fraternity.
- **Pledge/associate member**–a person who has accepted an invitation to join a fraternity/sorority.

- **Pledge trainer/new member educator**–the individual in charge of the pledge class, who is charged with preparing the pledges/new members for initiation.
- **Quota**–the maximum number of women a sorority may pledge for sororities participating in formal rush.
- **Recommendation**–a written letter or statement recommending a person to a chapter.
- **Ritual**–the formal document that contains the secret principles and ideals upon which groups were founded and which Greeks swear to uphold in their daily lives. It is shown to pledges at initiation; thereafter, it can be studied and used in chapter meetings.
- **Rush**–the time when fraternities and sororities recruit members, generally held in the fall semester.
- **Rushee**–a man or woman who is registered for rush and is attending rush functions.
- **Sister**–a term used by active members of a sorority or women's fraternity when referring to each other.
- **Sororities**–fraternities for women.

The week of rush can be overwhelming if you do not know what to expect. First of all, you can expect every other girl going through rush to be feeling the same way you do—lost, confused, and over-stimulated. You can expect that each house will know you by name and know everything you put on your high school resume you sent to them. You can expect lots of cheering, singing, skits, and conversations. In those sometimes awkward ten-minute conversations, take advantage of the opportunity to ask some great questions that will help you make a wise sorority decision:

- What do you like best about your sorority?
- How can new members get involved in sorority activities?
- Do you have any Bible studies or discipleship groups?
- What kind of extra-curricular activities do the girls in this chapter get involved in?
- What makes your sorority unique among all the others represented on campus?
- What are your favorite "hole-on-the-wall" restaurants in this town?
- Where are your favorite places to shop?

If you decide to go through rush, remember to be yourself and enjoy meeting the people each day in line. Soak in the fact that you will be getting a peek inside all the sorority houses, ponder in your heart how you feel about each different group of girls, and pray for God's direction each night. If you then decide to pledge a sorority, make the decision that's best for you. Not for your mom, not for your best friend, or even best for the new friends you made that week. Let the Lord lead you to the place where you will spend so much time during your college years, even if it's not in a sorority at all.

The irony of my entire sorority experience was that I went into the whole thing hoping, but ultimately skeptical, that I would find any good friends or even Christian friends. The truth and blessing was that my particular sorority was overflowing with believers. One of my roommates my sophomore year in the sorority house ended up discipling me while we were living together. I was more spiritually challenged and encouraged by those great women than I ever have been in my spiritual journey. For that, I am eternally grateful.

I encourage you to have an honest and open mind when it comes to the sorority scene. And by all means, if it's not for you, don't be afraid to say no. There are many other ways to find good friends on a college campus.

Chapter Seventeen Reflection Questions

1. What are your current opinions of sororities?

2. How familiar are you with the technical process of registering and the financial preparations required to go through rush?

3. Are you strong enough to make a stand and be a witness for Jesus Christ in an environment that is full of worldly temptations?

4. Can you be in a room where most everyone is drinking and, as an underage student, not drink?

5. Are you prepared to say no if, once invited in a sorority, you find that it is not going to be a place where you can grow spiritually?

Digging Deeper

■ Read through these verses and examine yourself before you decide whether or not to go through sorority rush:

- Galatians 1:10   Whom are you trying to please?

- James 5:8   Can you stand firm in your faith?

- Colossians 2:8   Are you easily deceived?

- Psalm 25:4-5   Have you prayed about it?

Chapter 18

THE DATING GAME

> Therefore, my dear brothers, stand firm. Let nothing move you. Always give yourselves fully to the work of the Lord, because you know that your labor in the Lord is not in vain.
>
> —1 Corinthians 15:58

There is a reason that romantic comedies hardly ever tank at the box office, that over 80 percent of the music industry sells songs about love, and that you probably skipped to this chapter long before you were this far into the book. We are all looking for love, and this becomes a very serious subject when you get to college. A recent survey revealed 83 percent of college-age women reported that marriage is an important goal and 63 percent of college-age women desire to find their husband while in college.[91] That is reason enough to take the dating game seriously when you exit high school and enter the college dating scene.

Dating God's Way

If dating for you is anything like it was living under my parents' roof, then you might find your dad cleaning his guns before your date comes to pick you up, your mom popping her head into the game room when you and your boyfriend are watching a movie to see if you "need anything," or your little sister hiding in the hall trying to catch a glimpse of any good-night kisses at the homecoming goodbye finale. You may be laughing at these, but they all actually happened to me. Looking back, I'm thankful they did for one simple reason: accountability.

One major piece of protection you don't realize you have right now is the accountability of having to be home by a certain hour, the "What did you do last night?" questions, and the pesky little siblings blabbing every move you make to your parents. Accountability isn't probably the word you would use to describe it, but knowing deep down that you have to answer those hard questions, be in by a certain hour, and possibly have someone watching you keeps you in check.

You see, your parents weren't doing these things to embarrass you, annoy you, or keep you from being "cool." They had one thing on their minds when you started dating...and that was to protect you from the overwhelming amount of sexual temptation surrounding you and every other teenager today.

Having an accountability partner during college is a great way to help keep these same ideas in check. With the number of marriages that come out of college dating relationships, it's not trite to have a few people on your team making sure you are after God's best.

To be totally honest, dating hasn't been around that long. The idea of dating and finding a mate in America has definitely evolved over the years, as explained by Natalie Flynn in "The Historical Evolution of Dating in America":

> American courtship began when America was first breaking ties with its mother country of England during the colonial period. Most of the customs of courtship revolved around rational needs and not lust. A man could only marry a woman if he could support a family with his income and possessions. Many believed that love developed only after a marriage progressed and not before. The seeking of a mate was not necessary because most couples knew each other from social activities, such as church.[92]

Our modern way of finding a life mate is radically different from that of colonial days. In light of our culture and the world in which we live, what are things to consider when dating—especially in college—away from our parents' approval and protection? Keep your standards high by asking a few of the following questions:

1. **First and foremost, is he a Christian?**

   If he is not, don't even think about it. Not being equally yoked is one thing the Bible is adamantly clear about (2 Corinthians 6:14-16). And as tempting as it is, don't try to justify "missionary dating" (otherwise known as getting involved in a relationship in hopes that you can lead him to Christ). As noble as that sounds, it's just dangerous. He should start off as (and later continue to be) the spiritual leader, not you.

2. **Who are his friends?**

   Spend time with him in groups and find out whom he hangs around. The company he keeps is a great indicator of what he might become.

3. **What is his reputation and character like?**

   Reputation is thought to be how other people perceive you…character is what you are in the dark when no one is watching. If the way you see him is totally different from how other people see him, take caution.

4. **Is he living a healthy lifestyle and willing to challenge you in all the areas we have discussed in this book?**

   You want to be with someone who can be a great encourager and motivator who makes you a better person. If he has an unbalanced life with many unresolved issues, then he can't lead you the way you deserve to be led.

5. **What are his long-term goals?**

    Or more specifically, are his passions and interests similar to yours? If your relationship progresses toward marriage, his life and your life will most likely be moving in the same direction. If his long-term plan is to blow his family's trust fund by traveling the world and opening his own fantasy football company, you might reconsider. You can sense pretty early if a guy has a solid work ethic and a good head on his shoulders.

6. **What are his sexual boundaries?**

    This could not be more important in a relationship. First, as believers, we are to keep ourselves pure until marriage. If he does not hold that same value, then run! Lots of things can happen before the act of sexual intercourse, so be sure you discuss early on your physical boundaries. If he does not respect you enough to have that conversation, then he won't respect you enough to stop when things are heated.

7. **Does he know how to set up a date, pick you up on time, and pay?**

    I know this seems weird, but it speaks highly of a guy when he has the guts to call you up, arrange an evening, pick you up when he says he will, and pay for the whole evening. This may sound old fashioned, but how a guy treats you during your dating years is a small glimpse of how he will treat you when you are married. If he doesn't call when he says he's going to call, doesn't respect your time, or expects you to foot most of the "entertainment" bills—then drop him like a hot potato. God wants the best for you, and you and I both know that is not the best way to treat a girl.

8. **Is he willing to do the pursuing, and are you willing to let him?**

Almost every Christian and secular book on dating will tell you that boys love a chase and a challenge. They want to be the ones to call you, to pursue you, and rescue you. When you step in and make it easy for them, they get confused and disinterested. Our culture has somehow perverted this idea and made this seem archaic.

9. **What do your parents think about him?**

Listening to the advice and counsel of godly parents is of utmost importance in a dating relationship, even if you are far away from home. If you are interested enough in dating a person, then try to arrange time for your parents and family to spend time with the two of you. Do the same with his family. Discovering how he connects and communicates with his own family will give you great insight into his personality, upbringing, and potential as a family man.

10. Have you prayed about it?

Before you go out with any guy or consider getting serious, make sure you have spent time praying about the situation. Ask God to give you clarity, discernment, and protection.

During the summer after my senior year of high school, my youth pastor Stuart Hall and his wife Kellee led a six-week study on dating, boyfriends, and future mates as we set off for college. Their motto was "Every date is a potential mate." That makes a lot of sense, and it is a great motto for you to carry into your college dating world as well. All these years later, I still have those notes. One of the biggest issues we discussed in that study was about being equally yoked. Take a look at Stuart and Kellee's excuse list below. Are you using any of these excuses to justify your relationship?

Excuses for Dating Non-Christians

- He understands me.
- He accepts me for who I am.
- I'm lonely.
- There aren't any Christians I want to date.
- Non-Christians have more fun.
- Christian guys are wimps.
- He's nicer than the Christian guys I know.
- He's really changing.
- I'm not going to marry him.
- I'll only go out with him once or twice.

- My friends think I should.
- Everyone will think I'm stuck up if I don't.
- I don't know how to say no to a non-Christian.
- I might lead him to Christ.

Dating as a Stronghold–Angela's Story

Angela didn't date much in high school and the few guys she did go out with were set-ups by friends or family. The boy who won most of her attention during her last year of high school was a boy her parents introduced to her. He was a football hero in their hometown, everyone loved his charismatic personality, and Angela was particularly drawn to his Matthew McConaughey abs. On top of it all, he professed to be a godly guy with pure intentions. Who wouldn't want to date this guy?

Somewhere between the first date and prom night senior year, Angela fell head over heels in love with him. Nothing he could say or do was wrong in her eyes. Even when he didn't call when he said he would call, was an hour late picking her up for homecoming, or his actions continually raised red flags to everyone around her—she was still convinced they would be together forever.

Somewhere during her senior year, she shifted all her security from her Lord to her boyfriend. When he didn't call when he said he would call, she got mad at everyone around her. When he didn't show up when he said he would show up, she cried to everyone around her. And when negative rumors about him made their way to her family, she put her fingers in her ears and justified everything for him. It got so bad, that during a late night cheerleading practice preparing for the NCA championships, Angela collapsed. Emotionally drained, spiritually empty, and physically down to a measly one hundred pounds (which is obviously dangerous for her 5'8" frame), she was hospitalized. Test results revealed that she had "mononucleosis," or mono, and she had nothing left in her to give.

As she lay in that hospital bed, God spoke to her heart and made her realize that she had put her hope in a person–and look where it had gotten her. He reminded her that He was the only one in whom she could place her faith and trust. Pulled from the performing squad due to her weak physical condition, Angela painfully cheered them on and watched her team win fourth in the nation that year—and all that after having to change the routine last minute due to her absence. She was embarrassed that she had allowed this person to rob her of her security, a fun senior year, possibly a national championship, and ultimately her health. To make things more complicated, both Angela and the young man somehow unknowingly picked the same college to attend. It wasn't until the end of her freshman year that she officially broke free from the emotional stronghold this person had over her. Angela's freedom did not come overnight, but through the Lord, it did come.

I present Angela's story not to tell you to break up with your high school sweetheart before you go to college, but to encourage you to do a security check. Where is your faith? You say it's in Jesus, but what would happen if you broke up with your boyfriend? Would it be the end of the world to you?

Dating (or Not) in College

Depending on the college you choose, you will most likely be surrounded by boys—new boys—who will be eager to take you out. Proverbs 4:23 says to "Guard your heart, for it is the wellspring of life." For me, that meant taking a dating break. I didn't expect it to last almost my entire college experience, but it was the best decision I made. Don't misunderstand, I liked boys…I really liked boys! But for the first time I had great guy friends I could be around without being in a relationship. *Just being friends with boys?* This was a new revelation for me.

This extreme decision is not for everyone, but take a moment and think about it. If you have a tendency to put your security in boyfriends rather than in Christ like Angela did, then consider the idea of taking a dating break your freshman year and enjoy both guy and girl friendships. Adjusting to college is hard enough; starting a serious relationship adds a whole different set of joys and struggles that can truly affect your freshman year. I'm not suggesting that you kiss dating goodbye, but the author of a thought-provoking book by a similar title ends with a great challenge:

Someday I'll have a story to tell. So will you. How will you respond when one day you look back on your love story? Will it bring tears of joy or tears of remorse? Will it remind you of God's goodness or your lack of faith in that goodness? Will it be a story of purity, faith, and selfless love? Or will it be a story of impatience, selfishness, and compromise? It's your choice. I encourage you (and continue to remind myself) to write a love story with your life that you'll feel proud to tell.[93]

What exactly are you supposed to be doing during all that time? Back to Stuart and Kellee's notes—a lot! Observe what a Proverbs 31 woman looks like when she's not out looking for a man:

How to Wait for the Right Guy Creatively without Getting Down in the Dating Dumps: Meet "Ruby" of Proverbs 31

1. Be a terrific teammate (Proverbs 31:11-12)
   What she projects: Looks at others' needs and offers support.
2. Cheerful worker (Proverbs 31:13)
   What she projects: Everything is done for the glory of God without complaining or arguing.
3. Great cook (Proverbs 31:14-15)
   What she projects: She is a good grocery shopper and cook.
4. Business woman (Proverbs 31:16)
   What she projects: Can handle overseeing a household and can manage money wisely.

COLLEGE BOUND ON SOLID GROUND

5. Exercise enthusiast (Proverbs 31:17)
   What she projects: Enjoys activity and stays in good physical shape.
6. Creative genius (Proverbs 31:18-19)
   What she projects: Uses her spiritual gift and isn't afraid to create. Her home is decorated and is a welcoming place for others.
7. Ministers to people (Proverbs 31:20)
   What she projects: She has a heart for the lost and for meeting other people's needs.
8. Fashionable dresser (Proverbs 31:21-22)
   What she projects: She buys modest clothes wisely. She can be in the world but not of it and can make a husband proud.

Hopefully, this information can give you a perspective on how to handle yourself and your time in and out of college while waiting for God's best. Becoming a Proverbs 31 woman is what God desires in all of us—whether we are married or not.

Let me end by saying that although many folks do end up finding a life mate during their college years, many do not. I was included in that latter crowd. It didn't really bother me until the first two years out of college when I was a single girl figuring out life in the real world and attending the wedding of a good friend every other weekend. I had always assumed that at that point in my life I would be not only engaged, but also married with a baby on the way. The truth was, nothing was missing. God had a plan for my life during those five years of singleness after college, and I am grateful for every one of them.

Do not fret and be desperate to find a husband in college. You may, and you may not find him there. Many of my friends did find their husbands in college and are living happily-ever-after lives today. I did not, and I'm also living a happily-ever-after story for my life. Consider this great passage from the book *Lady in Waiting*:

> One friend assumed that by going to a Christian college, she would inevitably find Mr. Right. Considering that she was from a very small town where more livestock lived than people, her strategy for finding a spouse seemed quite logical. She completed her four years and returned home without her "MRS." degree. Where do you think she found her mate? You guessed it, back in her very small hometown. God did not honor her logic, but He did honor her faith in Him to meet her needs.[94]

Waiting for the right one to come along can be tough at times, but it is so worth the wait! God created you and has a much better idea for a life partner than we could ever pick. "To marry a prince, you must first become a princess."[95] Enjoy your college days, and as a daughter to our King, focus first on becoming the princess Christ wants you to be. Don't let a silly thing like a boy control every move you make. If you find him in college—great. If you don't, the best is yet to come.

Chapter Eighteen Reflection Questions

1. As discussed in chapter ten, what are your physical/sexual boundaries when it comes to boys and dating?

2. Have you ever been in a relationship that had any kind of stronghold over you? Are you in one right now from which you need freeing?

3. What is your idea of how a guy should treat a girl?

4. Have you prayed for your future mate?

5. Are you willing to wait longer than your college years to meet that special someone?

Digging Deeper

■   Review these scriptures that align with the dating standards from earlier in the chapter. Fill in the blanks to remind yourself of things to be looking for in a godly man during a dating relationship.

    •   2 Corinthians 6:14-16
        Is he a _____?

- Proverbs 27:17
  Who are his _____?
- Proverbs 6:16-19
  What are his _____ and character like?
- Proverbs 10:17
  Is he living a _____ lifestyle?
- Proverbs 10:4
  What are his long-term _____?
- Song of Songs 2:7
  What are his _____ boundaries?
- Song of Songs 2:10
  Does he know how to set up a _____, pick you ____, and _____?
- Song of Songs 2:8
  Is he willing to do the _____, and are you willing to _____ _____?
- Exodus 20:12
  What do your _____ think about him?
- Colossians 4:2
  Have you _____ about it?

CONCLUSION

I will instruct you and teach you in the way you should go; I will counsel you and watch over you.

—Psalms 32:8

You are about to have the time of your life. I hope and pray that each day of college is full of joy and new adventures. All the uncertainties and anxieties you may have will soon dissipate, and not long from now you will be a full-blown college student! During this wonderful time, may you grow in wisdom, stature, and in favor with God and men. A balance in these four areas is certainly a lifelong journey, but I truly believe that college is the best place to begin putting these pillars into place. The next big transition for you will be from college to the real world. No one has to tell you it's a tough world these days.

Matthew 7:24-27 describes the difference in those who build their foundation on rock versus those who build their foundation on sand:

> Therefore everyone who hears these words of mine and puts them into practice is like a wise man who builds his house on the rock. The rain came down, the streams rose, and the winds blew and beat against that house; yet it did not fall, because it had its foundation on the rock. But everyone who hears these words of mine and does not put them into practice is like a foolish man who built his house on sand. The rain came down, the streams rose, and the winds blew and beat against that house, and it fell with a great crash.

My prayer is that as you begin this new phase of life, you will build it on solid ground. The storms will come and go, but with Christ as your rock, nothing can move you.

One of my pastors describes the Christian walk as being similar to a plant. It's either growing or dying. There's not really an in-between. Instead of suffocating your spiritual life during college, water it, nourish it, and be confident that God has great things in store for you. Really great things. Ruth and Warren Meyers beautifully convey this message in *Discovering God's Will*:

As the Master Designer of the Universe, God is all-wise. He knows all things. He's the one who thought up the complexities of space and the intricacies of the human cell. And He has in mind a good plan for your life, a plan that fits exactly your unique personality. His plan complements the calling He has in mind for you, with all He wants you to do and be. You and God's plan for you were conceived together in God's heart, tailor-made for each other. They're a perfect match.[96]

Roommates, sorority rush, dorm life, Bible studies, study groups, road trips, late nights, final exams, dropping classes, donating blood for the first time, voting for the first time, changing majors, making friends, going to date parties, making midnight Krispy Kreme runs, Frisbee golf, using a bike as your primary form of transportation, wearing lots of T-shirts, and ditching the make-up for a while are all a glimpse into your life in college. From books to boys and everything in between, your college years are years of promise, hope, and a whole lot of fun. I'll leave you with this famous and favorite quote of mine from the great movie *Shawshank Redemption*, "Either get busy living, or get busy dying."

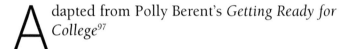

APPENDIX A
WHAT TO TAKE
TO COLLEGE

A dapted from Polly Berent's *Getting Ready for College*[97]

- Bible
- clothes
- lot of clothes hangers
- socks and underwear
- baseball cap for bad hair days
- raincoat/parka/umbrella
- boots (adventure and rain)
- laundry bag/basket/detergent
- quarters (lots!)
- small drying rack
- iron/tabletop ironing board
- regular (or extra long) twin sheets and pillowcases

- blanket
- pillows and comforter
- egg-crate mattress made out of foam
- towels and washcloths
- shower basket or caddy
- robe and flip-flops (shower shoes)
- toiletries
- hair accessories (dryer, straightener, curling Iron)
- medicine cabinet items
- fan and extension cords*
- desk light
- three-prong adapter
- small tool kit
- flashlight and batteries
- duct tape
- backpack or book bag
- dictionary and thesaurus
- calculator, batteries, stapler, ruler
- desk tray/divider
- stamps/stationery/envelopes
- calendar or planner
- message board for inside dorm room door
- cork board for outside dorm room door
- posters/pictures
- funtack (using nails in walls can sometimes get you fined)
- under-bed storage
- crates/stacking shelves
- bike and industrial strength lock

- beanbag chair or futon for extra seating (depending on space)
- carpet/floor mat
- stereo/iPod/alarm clock
- TV/DVD player
- answering machine
- camera
- computer and printer (plus five-plug outlet strip)*
- microwave/toaster oven*
- mini-refrigerator*
- coffeemaker/filters/coffee
- can/bottle opener
- dishwashing detergent
- plastic or acrylic plates, bowls, and cups
- silverware
- large bowl for popcorn
- chip clips
- portable vacuum cleaner
- cards/board games
- guitar
- favorite sports gear (rollerblades, Frisbee, basketball)
- sunscreen
- pepper spray

*Check with your school and dorm policies concerning all electrical equipment. Some may have strict regulations on appliances.

APPENDIX B
SAFETY TIPS
FOR STUDENTS

Adapted from *Girls Fight Back!: The College Girl's Guide to Protecting Herself* by Erin Weed[98]

Basic:

- Find out the security features on your campus (night guards, escort services, police stations, emergency blue phones).
- Find your campus crime statistics at www. securityoncampus.org.
- Do a search for sex offenders in your community.
- Get valuables insured.
- Give a copy of your class schedule and activity meeting times to your family and close friends.

- Program emergency numbers into your cell phone, including campus police, 911, your parent/guardian contact info and your ICE (In Case of Emergency contact) on your cell phone.
- LOCK YOUR DORM OR APARTMENT AT ALL TIMES!
- Create a list of emergency numbers and post them on the wall next to your phone in your dorm or apartment.

More Specific

- Go out with your girlfriends, and come home with your girlfriends.
- Convey strong body language when walking alone (good posture, free arm movement, and constant eye contact with those around you).
- Don't be afraid to use your voice and yell to set boundaries if someone uncomfortable approaches you.
- Do not let repairmen in your apartment or dorm without a roommate or friend over. Tell them through the door they will have to come back at another time.
- Make sure curtains or blinds cover your windows.
- Protect your identity online when ordering items, filling out applications, or posting personal information on MySpace or Facebook (don't give out too much information).

- Carry mace or pepper spray in your purse and in your car.
- Take a self-defense class!

APPENDIX C
101 CRAZY, FUN, AND RANDOM THINGS TO DO IN COLLEGE

Favorite memories from current and former college students:

1. Take road trips—to all nearby cities.
2. Flour fights instead of snowball fights (using flour and water…it gets gross).
3. Night rapelling off campus buildings.
4. Bubbles in the campus fountains.
5. Study abroad one summer or semester.
6. Cook a five-course meal with your roommate for friends.
7. Join a co-ed intramural team.
8. Go on a hunt for the best mashed potatoes in the city.
9. Go bowling in the middle of the day—or glow in the dark style in the middle of the night.

10. Sit in a park and eat a sack lunch on a beautiful day.
11. Pile as many girls in a dorm room as you can and start a movie marathon.
12. Go on a spring break ski trip at least once.
13. Go to every museum in the city and on campus.
14. Never pass an art gallery without one quick walk-through.
15. Challenge yourself to not drink soft drinks for a year.
16. Try every vegetable at the nearest farmers' market.
17. For one year use your bike as the only means of transportation.
18. Host a night of praise and worship in your apartment.
19. Dress up like *The Matrix* characters in all black patent leather for a day.
20. Promote a dorm contest to see who can go the longest without showering.
21. Go camping at least once.
22. Learn to play Frisbee golf and Ultimate Frisbee.
23. Host a "game night" in your dorm or apartment stocked with Trivial Pursuit, Catch Phrase, or Scene It.
24. Attend at least one play or show in the nearest town.
25. Attend at least one concert in the park.
26. Bury your roommate's dishes in her sheets if she doesn't clean them properly.

27. Take full advantage of Sonic's happy hour.
28. Drive around nearby neighborhoods and take a dip in every pool you see.
29. Meet with the student body president to learn of the ways you can get involved with campus activities.
30. Find your favorite coffee shop and go there at least once a week.
31. Find your favorite study spot on campus and never tell anyone where it is.
32. Read the Bible through in a year.
33. Play dress up and take pictures in the nearest thrift resale shops.
34. Take one weekend evening and stay up all night to watch the sunrise.
35. Attend at least one game or match of every sporting event on campus.
36. Reserve a college elective class to take something absolutely random.
37. Take a self-defense class.
38. Put a penny in a jar every time you study at an IHOP late at night.
39. Use a spring break or week in the summer to go on a mission trip.
40. If possible, ride the campus bus at least once.
41. Learn how to play a new instrument.
42. Host or attend dress-up parties.
43. When you see a high school student with her parents on campus, take a minute to talk with them and show them around.

44. Tutor students at a local elementary school.
45. Dance, dance, dance!
46. Start a Bible study with friends or classmates.
47. Call home at least once a week to check in.
48. Bring friends back to your hometown and show them your roots.
49. Go to your friends' hometowns and see their roots.
50. Attend a reputable Christian conference with a group of guys and girls.
51. Kidnap your friend on her birthday in the middle of the night.
52. Attend a mid-day matinee at the movie theatre.
53. Dress up like hillbillies (with "Bubba teeth" and all) and go shopping.
54. Walk or run in a 5K.
55. Put a new flower arrangement on your table every week.
56. Start a "spiritual marker" journal where you record the amazing things God teaches you during your college years.
57. Make a list of places you want to see before you die.
58. Try to visit at least three of those places during your college years.
59. Start a supper club.
60. Join a political campaign (either school wide, local, state, or national).
61. Vote.

62. Recycle cans and newspapers.
63. Contest a parking ticket.
64. Take at least one CLEP test and try to receive credit without having to take a class.
65. Write a letter telling your favorite teacher growing up how much you appreciate him or her.
66. Buy a mini-filing cabinet and start organizing bills and important documents.
67. Take a couples dance class with a trusted guy friend.
68. Carry extra testing scantrons and lend them out to those panicked students who forgot them on test days.
69. Tithe 10 percent of your money.
70. Take a picture of yourself with every statue on campus.
71. Read the newspaper.
72. Go canoeing on a nearby lake.
73. Make a college scrapbook that's ongoing for each year. If you don't do it while you're in college, you'll never do it.
74. Live one year without a TV in your room or apartment.
75. Learn to rollerblade.
76. Keep going to the dentist every six months (even if it is your hometown dentist).
77. Share your faith with someone.
78. Start a prank war with some guy friends:
    a. Put Orajel on their toothbrushes.
    b. Cover their toilets with plastic wrap.

    c. Put an opened can of tuna under someone's car seat.

    d. Tie their front door to a tree.

    e. Completely swap the furniture in the rooms of two friends.

    f. Place hundreds of Dixie cups with water on the floor of your buddies' dorm room.

    g. Create a "prize statue" or trophy that is passed back and forth when pranks occur.

79. At the end of your college experience, make a video with all your college friends, using your college pictures and give them out as graduation gifts.

80. Ask questions to soapbox speakers on campus.

81. Get a passport.

82. Host a block party or tailgate before a sporting event.

83. Leave encouraging notes on friends' message boards.

84. Go hitting at a batting cage.

85. Go putt-putting blindfolded.

86. Read a non-school related book a month.

87. Fly a kite.

88. Jump off the highest diving board on campus.

89. Buy a pocket-size Bible and keep it in your backpack.

90. Start a tradition with your roommates.

91. Invite your siblings to come stay with you one weekend.
92. Call your grandparents.
93. Learn to make your bed in less than sixty seconds.
94. Drink a bottle of water a day.
95. Donate blood.
96. Cover someone's dorm door with crazy colored post-it notes
97. Start working crossword puzzles.
98. Go Christmas caroling.
99. Toilet paper your friend's dorm room.
100. Write a thank you note to the person financially supporting your college experience.
101. Leave your mark—somehow, somewhere.

ENDNOTES

[1] Jacques Ellul, *Reason for Being: A Meditation on Ecclesiastes* (Grand Rapids, Michigan: Wm. B. Eerdmans Publishing Company, 1990), 282-83.

[2] Patricia M. McDonough, *The School-to-College Transition: Challenges and Prospects* (Washington D.C.: American Council on Education, Center For Policy Analysis, 2004), 5.

[3] Darrel Bock, *Jesus According to Scripture* (Michigan: Baker Academic, 2002), 74.

[4] Derek Melleby and Susan den Herder, "Navigating the College Transition," *Comment* magazine, February 2006–V 251.13 (Work Research Foundation, 2006),http://wrf.ca/comment/article.cfm?ID=173 (accessed January 4, 2007).

[5] Steven Garber, *The Fabric of Faithfulness* (Illinois: Intervarsity Press, 1996), 81.

[6] Abbie Smith, *Can You Keep Your Faith in College?* (Sisters. Oregon: Multnomah Publishers, Inc, 2006), 13.

[7] Kara Powell, "Where Do They Go Once They Graduate?" Center for Youth and Family Ministry, 2006, http://www.cyfm.

net/article_printer_friendly.php?article=Where_Do_They_Go_
Once_They (accessed January 4, 2007).

[8] Kara Powell and Krista Kubiak, "When the Pomp and
Circumstance Fades," *Youth Worker Journal,* September/October
2005, www.youthworker.com (accessed January 4, 2007).

[9] David Conley, "Rethinking the Senior Year," *National
Association of Secondary School Principals, NASSP Bulletin,* May
2001, www.findarticles.com/p/articles/mi_qa3936/is_200105/
ai_n8932918/print (accessed January 9, 2007).

[10] Randall S. Hansen, Ph.D, "High School Seniors: Preparing
for Your Next Step After High School," *Quintessential Careers*
http://www.quintcareers.com/printable/after_high_school.html
(accessed January 9, 2007).

[11] J. Budziszewski, *How to Stay Christian in College* (Colorado:
NavPress Publishing, 2005), 149.

[12] Katharine Hansen, "What Good is a College Education
Anyway? The Value of a College Education," *Quintessential
Careers,* www.quintcareers.com/printable/college_educa-
tion_value.html (accessed January 9, 2007).

[13] "Census Bureau Data Underscore Value of College Education"
U.S. Census Bureau News (U.S. Department of Commerce,
released October 26, 2006), www.census.gov (accessed January
9, 2007).

[14] Henry Blackaby, *God's Invitation: An Invitation to College
Students* (Lifeway Press, 1996), 51.

[15] "Women Boost Education Pace." *U.S. Census Bureau News*
(U.S Department of Commerce released June 29, 2004), www.
census.org (accessed January 9, 2007).

[16] "More Than 11 Million College Students Receive Financial
Aid," *U.S. Census Bureau News* (U.S. Department of Commerce,
released August 24, 2006), www.census.org (accessed January
9, 2007).

[17] "Secretary Spellings Announces Plans for More Affordable,
Accessible, Accountable and Consumer Friendly U.S. Higher

Education System" (U.S. Department of Education, released September 26, 2006), www.ed.gov (accessed January 9, 2007).

[18] Julie Bonnin, "Entrance Essentials," *Texas College Guide* (Texas Monthy Publishing, 2007), 17.

[19] Mary Ann Newbill, "A Balancing Act: Creating Your First-Term College Schedule," *My FootPath: Experts in College Admissions,* www.myfootpath.com/CollegeLife/Adjust.php (accessed January 17, 2007).

[20] *Advanced Placement Report To the Nation, 2006,* (College Board, 2006) Appendix A: AP Data at a Glance, 79.

[21] Charles Colson, *How Now Shall We Live* (Illinois: yindale House Publishers, 2007), 540.

[22] Polly Berent, *Getting Ready for College* (New York: Random House, 2003), 167.

[23] Greg Gottesman, Daniel Baer, and Friends, *College Survival, 7th Edition* (Thompson Peterson's, 2004), 63

[24] Laurence Shatkin, PhD, *90-Minute College Major Matcher* (Indiana: Jist Publishing, 2007), 8-9.

[25] See note 5 above, 75.

[26] Cal Newport, *How to Win at College* (Broadway, 2005), 85.

[27] Lev Vygotsky, *Thought and Language* (Cambridge: MIT Press, 1986).

[28] Priscilla Evans Shirer, *A Jewel in His Crown* (Chicago: Moody Press, 1999), 43.

[29] "Statistics: How Many People have Eating Disorders?" *Anorexia Nervosa and Related Eating Disorders, Inc.* Updated January 16, 2006, http://www.anred.com/stats.html (accessed February 1, 2007).

[30] "Eating Disorder Statistics" *About: Parenting of Adolescents,* http://parentingteens.about.com/cs/eatingdisorders/a/eating-disorder5.htm (accessed February 1, 2007).

[31] Gwen Shamblin, *The Weigh-Down Diet* (NewYork: Doubleday Publishing, 1997), 118-119, 48.

[32] Nanci Hellmich, "Freshman 15 Drops Some Pounds," *USA Today,* October 23, 2006, http://www.usatoday.com/news/health/2006-10-22-freshman-weight_x.htm (accessed January 4, 2007).

[33] See note 29 above.

[34] Daphine Oz, *The Dorm Room Diet* (New York: NewMarket Press, 2006), 71-72, 78-80.

[35] "College Students and Alcohol Abuse Statistics" *Healthy Minds. Healthy Lives* (American Psychiatric Association), http://www.healthyminds.org/collegestats_new.cfm (accessed February 5, 2007).

[36] "Drug Use: Youth, General Population, Workforce," *Bureau of Justice Statistics* (U.S. Department of Justice Report, 2004), http://www.ojp.usdoj.gov (accessed February 7, 2007).

[37] "High School to College Transition," *Pennsylvania Liquor Control Board,* Last Modified 3/28/2005 http://www.lcb.state.pa.us/edu/cwp.view (accessed January 1, 2007).

[38] David J. Hanson, Ph.D, "The National Minimum Drinking Age Act of 1984," *Alcohol: Problems and Solutions* Web site, http://www2.postdam.edu/hansondj/YouthIssues/1092767630.html (accessed February 7, 2007).

[39] "Underage Drinking and Drunk Driving Statistics Among College Students" *UMADD* Web site, www.umadd.com (accessed February 5, 2007).

[40] "Alcohol: What You Don't Know Can Harm You," *College Drinking Prevention* Web site, http://www.collegedrinkingprevention.gov/ (accessed February 5, 2007).

[41] See note 35 above.

[42] See note 39 above.

[43] See note 39 above.

[44] See note 39 above.

[45] See note 36 above.

[46] Daniel Whitfield, "Alcohol and the Bible" copyright 1999, http://chetday.com/alcoholandthebible.html (accessed March 20, 2007).

[47] Jackie Kendall and Debby Jones, *Lady in Waiting* (Pennsylvania: Image Publishers, 2005), 82-85.

[48] "The Truth About STDs," *Sexuality Information and Education Council for the United States* Publication, http://ww.siecus.org/pubs/fact/fact0019.html (accessed February 14, 2007).

[49] "Statistics: Sex in America," *Leadership U,* updated: June 13, 2002, htpp://www.leaderu.com/everystudent/sex/misc/stats.html (accessed February 14, 2007).

[50] "Trends in Reportable Sexually Transmitted Diseases in the United States, 2005," *Centers for Disease Control Publication,* December 2006, www.cdc.gov (accessed February 14, 2007).

[51] Diana Hagee, *The King's Daughter* (Nashville: Thomas Nelson Publishers, 2001), 120.

[52] See note 49 above.

[53] "The Truth About Adolescent Sexuality," *Sexuality Information and Education Council for the United States* Publication, www.siecus.org/pubs/fact/fact0020.html (accessed February 14, 2007).

[54] See note 47 above, 82-85.

[55] "College Sex & Love: Why Wait to Have Sex in Marriage?" *Iamnext* Web site, http://ww.iamnext.com/sexand (accessed February 14, 2007).

[56] See note 53 above.

[57] Paul Strand, "Generation Sex: Promiscuity Makes the Grade on Campus," *The Christian Broadcasting Network,* http://www.cbn.com (accessed February 14, 2007).

[58] Shannon Ethridge, *Every Woman's Battle* (Colorado: Waterbrook Press, 2003), 116.

[59] See note 57 above.

[60] See note 8 above.

[61] Rob Bell, *Nooma: Sunday,* (Michigan: Zondervan, 2005).

[62] A.W. Tozer, *The Pursuit of God* (Pennsylvania: Christian Publications, 1993), 17.

[63] C.S. Lewis, *Mere Christianity* (New York: Touchstone Publishing, 1952), 43.

[64] Donald S. Whitney, *Spiritual Disciplines for the Christian Life* (Colorado: Navpress Publishing, 1994).

[65] Howard Hendricks, *Living by the Book* (Chicago: Moody Press, 1991), 9.

[66] Ruth and Warren Meyers, *Discovering God's Will* (Colorado: Navpress, 2000), 23.

[67] Stormie Omartian, *The Power of a Praying Woman* (Oregon: Harvest House, 2002), 13.

[68] Becky Trabassi, *Let Prayer Change Your Life* (Nashville: Thomas Nelson Publishers, 1992).

[69] See note 64 above.

[70] Richard Foster, *Celebration of Discipline* (San Francisco: Harper, 1998), 47.

[71] Henry and Richard Blackaby with Claude King, *Experiencing God: Knowing and Doing the Will of God* (Tennessee: LifeWay Press, Revised 2007), 124.

[72] See note 62 above, 67.

[73] Sofield, Hammet, and Juliano, *Building Community* (Indiana: Ave Maria Press, 1998).

[74] Kelvin Smith, "Finding a Church: Your Home Away from Home," *Student Leadership Journal* (Intervarsity Fellowship, 2004).

[75] Steve Shadrach, "10 Top College Ministries in the U.S.," *Boundless Webzine,* http://www.boundless.org/regulars/list_guy/a0000859.html (accessed March 13, 2007).

[76] See note 5 above, 37.

[77] *Discover Your Life Ministry* (Highland Park Presbyterian Church, 2007).

[78] Bill Hybels and Mark Mittelberg, *Becoming a Contagious Christian* (Michigan: Zondervan, 1994), 123-132.

[79] Women of Faith Bible Study Series, *Celebrating Friendship* (Grand Rapids: Zondervan, 1998), 51.

[80] See note 5 above, 158.

[81] "Tips for Adjusting to University Life," *MIT Alumni Association* Web site, http://alum.mit.edu/ccg/parents/tips.html (accessed January 4, 2007).

[82] Julia Devillers, *The College Dorm Survival Guide* (New York: Three Rivers Press, 2006), 85-86.

[83] See note 4 above.

[84] See note 8 above.

[85] See note 79 above, 46.

[86] Haley DiMarco, *Mean Girls All Grown Up* (Michigan: Revell 2005), 147-148,166.

[87] See note 11 above, 23.

[88] Seaman, Barrett, *Binge: What Your College Student Won't Tell You* (New Jersey: Wiley, 2005), 43,91.

[89] Robert McGee, *The Search for Significance* (Nashville: Word Publishing, 1998), 55.

[90] See note 62 above,111.

[81] Norval Glenn and Elizabeth Marquart, "Hooking Up, Hanging Out, and Hoping for Mr. Right: College Women on Dating and Mating Today," *Institute for American Values*, 2001.

[82] Natalie Flynn, "The Historical Evolution of Dating in America," www.oberlin.edu/faculty/ndarling/transistion/group21/history.html (accessed March 13, 2007).

[93] Joshua Harris, *I Kissed Dating Goodbye* (Oregon: Multnomah Books, 1997), 228.

[94] See note 47 above, 40,55.

[95] See note 47 above, 55.

[96] See note 66 above, 2.

[97] See note 22 above, 4-6.

[98] Erin Weed, *Girls Fight Back!: The Girl's Guide to Protecting Herself* (Boulder Press, 2006), 47,69,70,120.

Printed in the United States
124808LV00001B/25-36/P